How to Save Big on Workers' Compensation

With Insights from Leading Industry Experts

Adam Friedlander

ISBN: 0615442293
ISBN-13: 9780615442297
Library of Congress Control Number:2011921284

Table of Contents

Dedication

This book is dedicated to...

My best friend and wife, Lisa, and my wonderful children, David and Allie. They gave meaning to the word *joy*.

To my parents, Bert and Judy. They are dear friends and incredible sources of love, wisdom, and support. My father is my mentor and sounding board.

To my exceptional associate and friend Cosmo Preiato and to the rest of the Friedlander Group Team. Together, we make a difference.

To the hardworking and conscientious professionals at the New York State Insurance Fund.

To our valued clients.

Foreword

In 1992, Friedlander Group formed its first of five Workers' Compensation Safety Groups underwritten by the New York State Insurance Fund (NYSIF). Over the past nineteen years our dedicated team of specialists has continuously improved our unique processes. As a result, thousands of clients in the retail, wholesale, restaurant, hotel, and oil dealer industries have saved a combined quarter billion dollars in premiums.

But more important, those employers earned hundreds of millions more from improved productivity, efficiencies, and profits that resulted from keeping their employees (their number one asset) working.

My goal is to share proven and actionable money-saving ideas and insights that enable employers to operate at optimal levels.

The balance of the book includes interviews with leading workers' compensation experts, and together we offer insightful cost-saving ideas from a variety of perspectives. The experts include Larry LaPointe, former director of the Division of Confidential Investigations at NYSIF; Ed Hiller, director of Claims and Medical Operations for NYSIF; Brian Mittman, the managing partner of Markhoff & Mittman, PC, a law firm helping injured workers; Robert Firmbach, a veteran loss-control and safety expert; Eileen Preiato, the Friedlander Claims Solution™ manager; and Cosmo Preiato, executive vice president of Friedlander Group and head of Safety Group Underwriting and Operations.

As a point of reference, the appendix shares an overview of the unique processes of Friedlander Claims Solution.™

Maximizing the productivity of your number one asset, your employees, is the ultimate source of profits, and the ensuing savings on your workers' compensation is the icing on the cake.

Chapter 1

Winning Your World Series by Keeping Your Number One Asset Working

If Derek Jeter and Alex Rodriguez of the New York Yankees were injured during an October game and out for the season, do you think that the Yankees' management would be more concerned with the impact on their workers' compensation premium or their loss of revenue from not winning the World Series?

The Yankees understand that their employees are their number one asset and that they must keep them working and healthy to win. It's crystal clear for the Yankees, but not for most employers.

Managing workers' compensation costs is important, but the big money is in keeping employees working to maximize your organization's productivity, efficiencies, and profits (PEP).

Can you win your World Series without your team working optimally?

The path to keeping your employees working is through safety. Safety is a by-product of an organizational "culture of caring."

A culture of caring is created and nurtured by top management. From the president on down, the message must be made clear that management cares about the well-being of their employees. Employees must feel that their managers want them to go home from work in the same health in which they arrived.

Management must eliminate those unsafe actions and conditions that cause claims. They should analyze past claims, isolate patterns, and then eliminate the causes. This is the core function of a company's safety committee.

What Goes Around Comes Around

Employees appreciate knowing that management cares about their health and their ability to provide for themselves and their family.

Companies that effectively communicate their care for employees, where safety is an integral part of the culture, have fewer claims, less fraud, lower premiums, and increased productivity and profits. Everybody wins!

But it can go the other way too. Organizations with an abundance of claims usually have a management problem. They may lack an understanding of the need for safety, and management may be unaware of the self-defeating consequences.

Just as a culture of safety is contagious, so is one of disinterest and neglect. Employees may respond in kind and retaliate in very costly ways.

The costs to an organization generated by injured employees extend far beyond increased premiums. Premium costs represent an estimated one-quarter of overall injury expenses. Indirect costs include overtime, temporary labor, increased training, production delays, increased stress, property or equipment damage, and lower morale. These costs multiply as the culture moves in the wrong direction.

A Lightning Rod

Workers' compensation is a lightning rod. Many employers have a visceral reaction to workers' compensation that is out of proportion to the expense. Relative to other expenses, like payroll, rent, and cost of goods, it's small. Yet, for employers, it feels like having a pebble in their shoe.

Many employers think claims are "beyond their control" or that "most claims are fraudulent," or they simply resent the high premiums. Some erroneously conclude that claims are not their problem, thinking that "that's why we pay premiums" and spitefully "let the carrier pay." They stew over what they consider another unfair tax.

It's also a political football. Workers' compensation intersects the varied interests of employers and labor unions in addition to the medical, pharmaceutical, legal, and insurance industries.

That's why governors, including Mario Cuomo, George Pataki, Eliot Spitzer, and Arnold Schwarzenegger made the reform of workers' compensation a leading position of their platforms. They promised lower premiums to retain and attract employers to their states for tax revenues and employment. Conversely, labor unions and others seek larger benefits for their constituents, which increases premiums.

These conflicting agendas leave many feeling shortchanged and angry.

Chapter 2

Establishing a Culture of Caring

Creating a culture of caring for your employees' well-being is the single most important step in saving money on your workers' compensation. That culture will maximize your productivity, efficiencies, and profits (PEP Maximizer™). A culture of caring is the secret to optimizing performance as an organization.

But the proof is in the pudding. Top management's message of caring must be communicated by actions, not just words.

It begins with the interview process, who's hired, who's fired. It's reinforced by safety training, safety contests, safety inspections, claims-trend analysis, safety committee accountability, safety posters, injury management, local health-care provider relationships, and light-duty options that enable employees to return to work sooner.

"What gets measured gets done." When employees work together with management to eliminate unsafe acts and conditions, claims decline and profits increase.

My purpose here is to help ensure *that* you create a culture of caring. *How* you do so will be up to you and your partners in safety, including your insurance carrier and broker or consultant.

The good news is that safety is largely intuitive. People know that wet floors, poorly stacked boxes, dull knives, defective ladders and stairways, and heavy lifting can cause accidents and injuries. Many claims can be avoided if more attention is paid to detail, problems are anticipated, and safety is brought into focus organizationally. Safety committee members should be required to take responsibility for safety awareness and auditing.

Safety will be improved, for example, with driver screenings and training on proper lifting techniques, handling of chemicals, and the importance of wearing proper safety goggles and shoes. Fortunately, a large selection of safety videos is available as are experienced safety consultants who can provide on-site training.

As employees participate in training classes, they receive the underlying message that management cares about their safety. They will appreciate that their management "talks the talk and walks the walk."

Before working with us, one large employer had seventy claims totaling $1 million over five years. He didn't realize the magnitude of his problem until his claims data was consolidated in a simplified format. He quickly understood that his costs were huge to retrain, rehire, and deal with bad morale and the loss of productivity. Large premium increases motivated the employer to improve safety. Since focusing on safety, claims are down by 60 percent and the savings are significant.

Here, some clients share their culture of caring and safety success stories:

"As a fire department, we did not respond regularly to EMS calls prior to my becoming chief. After I took over, we started responding to EMS calls to assist the police department, which is the primary EMS agency. Within the first two months, we had three back injuries that resulted in comp. claims. I realized that the problem might be a training issue with the proper use of the stretchers and stair chairs. I had the police come in and do a training session on the proper techniques for using the stretcher and, more importantly, the stair chair. Since that time, we have not had any additional back injuries." —Chief Ed Rush, Hartsdale Fire Department, Hartsdale, NY

"Safety for our company is the same as security—a constant mind-set. Starting at the top, our culture stresses safety and security for our staff. We begin by including everyone in the process. "Pick up after yourself. Be personally responsible for your actions and don't put someone else in danger because of your inaction or laziness. Treat others as you wish to be treated." This permeates the entire organization; it transcends all levels of operation including customer relations. It is not lip service but a deliberate conscious action on the part of the principal person (in this case me) in the company to make sure that this mind-set is in every action carried out by this organization. There is no wiggle room. Anyone who does not buy into the culture is out."—Peter Longo, Porto Rico Importing Co., New York, NY

"My company has taken a proactive stance with delivery drivers. One rule that is taken very seriously is "The No Backup Policy." Drivers pull in to clients' locations and they pull forward right out. Another rule is "No cell phones in the trucks while driving." Those two rules alone work great for us."—Fred Marino, Olympia Auto and Truck, Lake Placid, NY

"I was so happy to receive our dividends this year for having a safe workplace record. We are diligent in training our staff to practice safe working habits. Our employees are quick to clean up any spills or debris on the floor. We also purchase nonslip shoes for our staff and require all staff members to wear them, including management. This has literally stopped injuries due to slips and falls. We teach safe lifting practices as well as using caution when behind another employee. With just these changes, we have reduced work-related accidents. We look forward to another successful year of keeping our employees safe."—Mina DeRenzo, Owner, Maple Lawn Dairy, Elmira, NY

"One thing that has worked out well is buying light-weight garbage bags instead of heavyweight. This stops employees from overloading the bags and injuring their backs lifting them. Essentially, if you put more than thirty pounds in the bags they will break."—Thomas Pane, The Grapevine Restaurant and Catering, Amherst, NY

These real-world examples of caring and safety are the keys to savings. Once a culture of caring is established and problems are exposed, any business can immediately improve. Maximizing productivity and profits and capturing workers' compensation savings are within management's control.

Unfortunately for employers, the insurance industry falsely concludes that since workers' compensation is statutory, innovative services will not add value. Actually, workers' compensation is more like rocky road ice cream masquerading as vanilla. The nuances are underestimated. This is a very costly misperception for employers, and I'll show you why.

Chapter 3

The Experience Modification

Insurance is purchased to transfer risk from the insured to the insurance carrier. However, due to the "boomerang effect" of what's called the workers' compensation experience modification, the costs of claims are ultimately charged back to the insured retroactively.

Each employer's workers' compensation premium is modified by the employer's claims experience, if the premium exceeds $5,000 annually. An *experience modification* is calculated by comparing an employer's actual claims for the prior three years to their expected claims for their specific payroll amount and industry classification. If an employer's actual claims' cost is more than expected, an additional premium is charged. But if the cost is less than expected, there's a reduction in premium.

Workers' compensation insurance only smoothes the adverse impact claims have on cash flow. The insurance carrier processes the claims but recoups the cost by applying an experience modification charge to the employer's premium. Consequently, risk is not transferred.

For smaller claims, below $10,000, many employers will actually pay *more* than the claim's cost as a result of their experience modification's impact on their premiums. Only on severe claims is the risk actually transferred to the insurance carrier.

Experience modifications can also be a source of savings for safety-conscious employers, if the costs of actual claims are less than expected. Unfortunately, most employers don't understand how their experience modification works and how they capture savings through safety.

Experience modifications range from up to a 40 percent discount to a 100 percent additional premium. That swing of 140 percent is no joke. Employers should carefully investigate what services are offered by insurance carriers and brokers to improve safety.

Most employers shop their workers' compensation, hoping to save 10 to 20 percent of their premium. Those savings are insignificant when compared to a potential 100 percent increase in experience modification. That's why focusing on safety and employees' well-being is so important.

How You Profit from Safety

A New York company's experience modification is calculated annually by the New York Compensation Insurance Rating Board and follows an employer regardless of the insurance carrier chosen. Outside of New York, the National Council of Compensation Insurance and other independent bureaus calculate experience modifications.

Each claim is included in three years of experience modification calculations. For example, an experience modification that is effective in 2010 will include claims amounts from 2008, 2007, and 2006. The prior year, in this case 2009, is never included.

As you can see in the chart below, the year 2008 is included in the 2010, 2011, and 2012 experience modifications.

	Experience Modification Year		
	2010	**2011**	**2012**
Claims Year	**2008**	2009	2010
	2007	**2008**	2009
	2006	2007	**2008**

Each claim has an impact on three years of experience modifications.

The impact of employers' claims experience, for better or worse, varies with the size of their annual premium, as illustrated below.

Three-Year Premium Cost of Various Claims[1]

Claim Amount	$10,000 Premium	$100,000 Premium	$500,000 Premium	$1,000,000 Premium
$500	71%	168%	180%	360%
$1,000	71%	168%	180%	360%
$5,000	71%	168%	189%	378%
$10,000	38%	95%	125%	249%
$50,000	11%	36%	73%	146%
$100,000	8%	29%	67%	134%

The chart shows the premium increases on various claims, charged as a percentage of the claim amount and paid over three years due to the claim's inclusion in the experience modification calculation for three years.

The retroactive charges for a claim increases as an employer's premium increases. For example, on a $10,000 premium, a $1,000 claim will cost 71 percent, or $710, billed over three years through the experience modification of premium.

Look at what happens to an employer with a $1 million workers' compensation premium. On a $1,000

---

1   Source of data is ModMaster, Specific Software Solutions, LLC

claim, the employer pays 360 percent, or $3,600, in additional premium over three years. Even on a $100,000 claim, the employer still pays 134 percent, or $134,000, in additional premium!

As annual premiums increase, claims must be larger before workers' compensation insurance shares in the cost and risk is successfully transferred. An employer with a $100,000 premium needs claims over $9,000 before their insurance pays a small portion of the claim.

In fact, on a $1 million premium, there is no risk transfer unless a claim increases after the three years is included in the experience modification calculation. In that case, there's no chargeback to the employer, and the insurance carrier is responsible for the payment.

Are You Sitting Down?

It gets worse. The Three-Year Premium Cost of Various Claims chart, in the preceding section, is the *best-case* scenario.

When claims are reported, the insurance company establishes *reserves* for the estimated ultimate cost of a claim. The estimate, or reserve, is used in the experience modification calculation and is usually higher than the final amount paid. For example, a claim that ultimately cost $3,000 could have an average reserve of $5,000 over four years before it closed. On a $100,000 premium, the employer would pay 168 percent of the $5,000 reserves included in the calculation, or $8,400 in additional premium for a claim that cost $3,000. Until a claim is "closed" and fully paid, the experience modification is based on reserves.

To be fair, reserving is not an exact science. Sometimes claims' reserves are significantly underestimated, and employers are spared the full impact from their experience modification.

As we will see in future chapters, there are several proven methods to reduce premiums including self-paying certain claims to keep them out of the system and reducing the reserves on open claims. You may need to hire an advocate who specializes in these services to capture the savings.

Your Minimum Experience Modification

Every employer should know what their minimum experience modification could be if the employer remained claim-free during the three years included in the calculation. The difference between an employer's current experience modification and its minimum is *the controllable experience modification.*[2]

For example, if an employer had a $500,000 premium before applying their experience modification (see the following chart), the difference between the current modification (1.15) and their minimum modification (.59) is the "controllable mod." of (.56). The difference between the employer's current modified

2   ModMaster, Specific Software Solutions, LLC

premium of $575,000 and their minimum modified premium of $295,000 is a savings of $280,000 in just one year alone. That's what I'm talking about.

The savings captured by minimizing your experience modification through safety, not to mention the ensuing improvements in your PEP, easily pays for your investment in safety.

Premium before Mod.	$10,000	$100,000	$500,000
Current Mod.	1.15	1.15	1.15
Current Premium	$11,500	$115,000	$575,000
Minimum Mod[3].	0.91	0.75	0.59
Minimum Premium	$9,100	$75,000	$295,000
Controllable Mod.	0.24	0.40	0.56
Controllable Savings	$2,400	$40,000	$280,000

By focusing on safety and by building a culture of caring, employers can capture all or part of their controllable mod. Maximizing productivity, efficiencies, and profits will be a very worthwhile and motivating goal for your team to achieve.

---

3   Source of Data is ModMaster, Specific Software Solutions, LLC

Chapter 4

Cost-Saving Products and Partners

Once management commits to building and nurturing a Culture of Caring™ Company, the next step is finding partners who can help you maximize your safety and capture savings on your workers' compensation.

Since most insurance consultants and brokers do not specialize in workers' compensation, you will need to do some research to find the right partners.

The same is true for insurance companies. Most carriers do not offer the services needed to take your company to the next level. Part of the problem for insurance carriers is that workers' compensation insurance has historically been a money loser for them. Claims and operating expenses have exceeded premiums.

However, there are brokers, consultants, and insurance carriers that add value with a variety of specialized claims administration and loss-control services. An outline of cost-saving and value-added services provided by Friedlander Group is included in the appendix of this book as a point of reference. The right partners make a significant difference, especially for larger employers where the experience modification is more costly. The savings from reduced experience modifications more than justify the investment in safety.

Once a broker or consultant who specializes in workers' compensation safety and claims administration is chosen, you'll want to select a policy that rewards you for safety. A *loss-sensitive* workers' compensation policy offers savings and dividends to employers with low claims. However, until your claims are under control, a guaranteed cost plan might be more appropriate. A guaranteed cost premium will not change regardless of claims experience, other than changes from the experience modification.

There are basically two low-cost options in the New York marketplace. The first is a well-run safety group, underwritten by the New York State Insurance Fund (NYSIF), and the second is a loss-sensitive dividend-paying plan from standard carriers.

Formed in 1923, the NYSIF Safety Group Program currently consists of 102 safety groups that include most industries. Safety groups spread risk among employers in the same industry that have track records of safety and low claims. Members receive advance group discounts, and the profits, if any, are paid back in the form of an annual dividend. In 2009, the NYSIF safety groups paid an average dividend of 30 percent, totaling $177 million.

Factors to consider when choosing a safety group are the dividend history of the group; the size and growth of the group; the size of the savings or contingent balance, which is used to fund future dividends and increases in claims; and the services provided by the group manager.

NYSIF is a *not-for-profit* insurance company, which is a fundamental reason that a well-run safety group can pay significant dividends. Members receive what standard carriers keep: the profits.

The unique benefits of a NYSIF safety group are structural features: the product has low expenses and operates on a not-for-profit basis, performance risk is spread over safety-conscious members, members are fully insured, and maximum cost is guaranteed. Each member receives the same dividend regardless of its claims for that dividend period. Even if your company had an unusually bad claims year, the performance of the group is what determines your dividend.

The chart below shows the paid dividend history of the safety groups managed by the Friedlander Group. The dividends were in addition to an average 25 percent advance group discount.

$123 Million Dividends Paid - Friedlander Group

		Retail Group of NY #544	Wholesale Group of NY #551	United Restaurants of NY #556	Hotels/ Motels of NY #578
	Inception Dates	3/1/92	4/1/93	9/30/93	6/1/06
1	1992-93	30%			
2	1993-94	32.5%	30%	30%	
3	1994-95	32.5%	32.5%	37.5%	
4	1995-96	35%	35%	52.5%	
5	1996-97	50%	42.5%	52.5%	
6	1997-98	60%	50%	40%	
7	1998-99	45%	45%	45%	
8	1999-00	30%	35%	40%	
9	2000-01	32.5%	32.5%	25%	
10	2001-02	32.5%	25%	27.5%	
11	2002-03	35%	30%	35%	
12	2003-04	35%	32.5%	40%	
13	2004-05	35%	35%	40%	
14	2005-06	35%	35%	35%	
15	2006-07	30%	30%	35%	25%

16	2007-08	35%	35%	40%	25%
17	2008-09	35%	30%	40%	25%
18	2009-10	35%	25%		
		36.4%	**34.1%**	**38.4%**	**25%**
		18-year average	17-year average	16-year average	3-year average

The Average of 54 Dividends is 36%

Loss sensitive policies can also pay dividends, but the dividend is based exclusively on the claims experience of the individual insured. The risk is not spread. An employer needs very low claims in order to outperform a safety group. Since "claims happen," a well-run safety group usually offers a better risk–reward alternative.

There are other alternative products like self insurance and "captives," but a well-run safety group offers higher savings and a guaranteed maximum cost.

Chapter 5

Interview with Larry LaPointe, Director of Confidential Investigations, NYSIF

Mr. Larry LaPointe has over thirty years of experience in the investigation and prosecution of white-collar crime, with particular emphasis on insurance fraud. He is currently an attorney in private practice.

Mr. LaPointe served as the director of the Division of Confidential Investigations at the New York State Insurance Fund (NYSIF) from March 1998 until his retirement from public service in August 2010. In addition to directing a staff of thirty-five investigators, attorneys, and support staff, Mr. LaPointe and his staff conducted a comprehensive, continuing examination of the Fund's business processes to ensure that workers' compensation fraud would be detected, documented, and responded to in an effective manner. During his tenure, criminal prosecutions for fraud against NYSIF increased by 400 percent. Investigations initiated under his leadership have resulted in savings to NYSIF in excess of $160 million, making the Fund an industry leader in workers' compensation fraud investigation in New York.

Mr. LaPointe spent eleven years as an assistant district attorney in Suffolk County, New York, where he served as a deputy chief of the Rackets Bureau, and at various times supervised the White Collar Crime Unit and the Civil Forfeiture Unit. Among his accomplishments as a prosecutor were the planning and direction of two highly successful videotaped undercover sting operations that resulted in the prosecution of over one hundred individuals for insurance fraud, stolen property, narcotics, and weapons offenses.

After leaving the district attorney's office, Mr. LaPointe served as the director of the Revenue Crimes Bureau at the New York State Department of Taxation and Finance, where he was in charge of all criminal investigations involving corporate, income, and sales tax. Among his accomplishments were long-term investigations leading to three successful high-profile prosecutions, each of which involved excess of $1 million in taxes and penalties.

Before joining NYSIF, Mr. LaPointe served as the director of the Insurance Frauds Bureau at the New York State Insurance Department. In this position, he oversaw a significant expansion of the bureau's staff and the creation of a number of new specialized investigative units. He was also involved in the development of state legislation, which now requires insurance companies to create and implement comprehensive plans for fighting insurance fraud and to establish investigation units. During his tenure criminal prosecutions for insurance fraud and related crimes increased by 140 percent.

Adam: Larry, thank you for your participation. Let's start with what is fraud?

Larry: Fraud in workers' compensation is any transaction which seeks to deceive the Board or the insurance carrier, which results in a monetary loss. It could take the form of a worker filing a false claim with respect to an accident that didn't happen or attempting to turn an off-the-job injury into an on-the-job injury. It could take the form of a health-care provider billing for services that weren't rendered, and it can take the form of a business providing false information to the insurance carrier in order to get a lower rate for workers' compensation insurance, so it can take a whole number of different forms.

Adam: Why should an employer care about fraud?

Larry: Fraud costs money. When a worker goes out on workers' compensation, it's going to cause an increase in your rates. That injury has to be paid for; that claim has to be paid out. Fraud also costs money when your competitors are committing fraud with respect to their premiums and putting themselves in an economically advantageous position in which they can compete against your company and underbid you because they are not paying the proper rates for insurance.

Adam: What percent of premium does fraud account for?

Larry: It's very hard to tell. I think there is a wide variation, but the literature on the subject indicates that the construction industry is rife with premium fraud and that some of the other parts of the industry where the rates are lower, such as retail, have much less premium fraud. So, as a rule of thumb, the higher the rate, the more likelihood there is that fraud is involved in a premium.

Adam: What motivates people to commit fraud?

Larry: People commit fraud for a number of reasons. Workers commit fraud sometimes because they are having problems on the job and this is a way out of working for their employer without losing all of their income. Sometimes it's because they have an off-the-job injury and they don't have health-care coverage through the job; workers' compensation will provide them with payment for the operation that they need because of what happened off the job. Sometimes it will be a legitimate injury, and the person just gets used to not working because there isn't a strong return-to-work program in place to get them back to work, and the person kind of falls into fraud. With respect to businesses, they seem, in many cases, to be simply going too far in terms of cost cutting. Businesses, of course, want to be competitive so they want to keep costs down. There is a line you can't cross with respect to that; you can't lie about the risk; you can't lie about the size of your payroll. Once you do, you're committing a felony.

Adam: What are the current penalties for fraud?

Larry: There are a number of different penalties. There is a class E felony called workers' compensation fraud, which is punishable by up to four years in prison. There is also fraud crime, which is called insurance fraud, which is keyed to the amount of the premium that was stolen or the amount of the money paid out by the carrier that was taken. Workers' compensation fraud can go as high as a class B felony, punishable by as much as twenty-five years in prison.

Adam: What percentage of cases result in convictions?

Larry: The experience across the board for all insurance carriers who have active programs is about a 90 percent conviction rate. That's because insurance carriers are very careful and selective in what cases they present the prosecutors and only present cases which are very strong.

Adam: What percentage of those convicted actually go to jail?

Larry: In New York, the likelihood of going to jail on a first offense workers' compensation fraud case is very small. I would say that in New York, less than 5 percent see jail time at all.

Adam: Do you see many repeat offenders?

Larry: We've seen a few, but that's rare. For a businessperson or worker, it's a shock being put in handcuffs, taken out of their house, taken to a police station, being processed, being put in a tank, being arraigned, having to hire a lawyer, and paying thousands of dollars for that. Plus, the economic penalties that are imposed, even on a non-jail sentence, are such that usually, if you've gone through that experience, you don't want to go through that again.

Adam: Have you found that the increased penalties have been helpful in fighting fraud?

Larry: In fighting fraud, I believe they have been helpful because the maximum penalty sends a signal. The maximum penalty is always possible. And if a defendant won't make a reasonable settlement with the prosecutor and makes the mistake of going to trial, I've seen people who thought that workers' compensation fraud wasn't a serious matter actually go to prison after trial.

Adam: Once people are convicted, they're convicted felons?

Larry: That's correct. You have a criminal record. You can no longer answer "no" on that question. And it's a difficult position, especially for a businessperson to be in, to have that record. These cases invariably get picked up by the press. Your entire community will know, your kids will know, their friends will know, and the people in your community will know. It's not a place that a business person wants to be.

Adam: I read about a conviction of an employer who understated payroll by $35,000 to save $2,400 in premium. Is that person now a convicted felon?

Larry: Sure, that happens quite frequently. Once you get past minimal amounts of "shaving your premium" into significant losses for the insurance company, a fraud is a fraud is a fraud. And you're going to get charged with a felony, and the likelihood is that you will be convicted of either a felony or a misdemeanor.

Adam: Has the probability of getting caught improved?

Larry: I think it has. Insurance companies in general are starting to pay more attention to workers' compensation then they did in the past. They are taking this matter more seriously, and they have learned that they can get cooperation from police and prosecutors to get these cases persecuted. So, yes, there is more of a chance that the cases are going to be detected, and they are going to be referred for prosecution.

Adam: What do you think is more of a deterrent, the stiffer penalties or an increased probability of being caught?

Larry: Probably the increased probability of being caught.

Adam: Are the stiffer penalties and increased probability of being caught being communicated to the public?

Larry: The law in New York requires insurance companies to have a public information program. And some insurance companies pool together through associations, and they have Web sites, and they take out print ads and radio and television ads on an annual basis to publicize the fact that this a serious matter and that you can go to jail for this as well as have a criminal record. So, yes, there is a lot being done to publicize it. But one always wonders how much of it gets through all of the media noise and actually registers on a particular businessperson or a particular employee.

Adam: What is the most common fraud?

Larry: The most common fraud is a claims fraud by a worker who started out with a legitimate claim, then secretly went back to work elsewhere and continued to collect.

Adam: Do you find that these workers are paid off the books or on the books?

Larry: Most commonly they are being paid off the books, not on the books. And that's being done intentionally as a way of hiding the fact that they have an income that they haven't reported as they should have.

Adam: If they were being paid on the books, is there interagency cooperation that would expose that situation?

Larry: If they are being paid on the books, there is an agreement between the Workers' Compensation Board and the Tax Department for a data exchange with respect to new hires who are being hired on the books. This helps to allow detection of a new hire on the books who is also collecting comp. So data exchange there helps with that.

Adam: Do higher benefits levels increase fraud?

Larry: Yes, because there is less incentive to go back to work. If you can get close to the maximum benefit and you can then start your dream business or get another source of income, part-time or full-time off the books, there are cases where people are now pulling down more income than they could if they honestly went back to work.

Adam: Which type of fraud is the most expensive?

Larry: Most expensive fraud is premium fraud. That's simply because in the higher risk categories, the rates of insurance are so high that the fraud amount adds up very quickly.

Adam: What is the track record of the New York State Insurance Fund (NYSIF) with respect to fraud, and how does it compare to the rest of the industry?

Larry: Well, I'm a former employee of NYSIF. I retired from NYSIF. I can't speak for them officially anymore, but I can tell you that during my tenure, NYSIF was, and to my knowledge continues to be, the industry leader in criminal fraud investigation and the industry leader in terms of the volume of investigations and successful prosecutions that result from their work.

Adam: In a case, what evidence do you need to feel that the odds are in your favor? If there's a 90 percent conviction rate, then what type of case is chosen to reach that conviction rate?

Larry: It depends upon what kind of crime we're talking about. If it's a claimant and they're on the books working with the Insurance Frauds Bureau and the Fraud Inspector General, if we have an idea of where they are working, those agencies have the ability to subpoena payroll records from the new employer, which will make a solid case of fraud. Nothing is better than payroll records to show that the person is making more than permitted before benefits start to be reduced. If the person is off the books, videotaping is very commonly used in the industry as a way of showing a number of things. It shows (a) that the person is working, and it very often shows (b) that the degree of injury that the person has alleged to the Board is exaggerated. And those are a strong basis on which to base a prosecution against an individual claimant. With respect to policyholders, these are classic white-collar paper cases. And the way that they're built is by developing a profile of the company. Who are their business partners? What volume of business do they do with their customers? What evidence can we develop as to the size of their payroll? These are very similar to tax fraud cases, and it's been my experience that quite often people who are committing premium fraud are also committing tax fraud.

Adam: What is the biggest obstacle encountered when prosecuting fraud?

Larry: It's changing, but historically, it has been getting law enforcement prosecutors to accept jurisdiction and authorize the prosecution on these cases. Over the course of time, with a lot of effort, prosecutors and courts are starting to take these cases more seriously. I would be happier if New York were more in line with other states in terms of the likelihood of doing jail time, but we're not there yet. That's going to take more time and more education.

Adam: What do you think employers should know about fraud?

Larry: They need to know that they have opportunities to protect themselves from fraud committed by their employees. A lot has to do with establishing a culture in their companies that encourages employees to take pride in their work, to enjoy their work, and to feel some sense of loyalty to the team that they work with. The second thing that employers can do to minimize fraud is to have a well thought out early-return-to-work program in place, if they can do that given the size of the business that they're in. If they can afford to do that, if they can afford to set it up, and if they have the resources, they should do it. Because the sooner you can get an injured worker back to work on any basis, the less likely a claim is to go from being legitimate to fraudulent.

Adam: Do you find that claimants don't start out with the intent to be fraudulent but fall into a fraudulent situation over time?

Larry: Habit is a fundamental human characteristic, and when you get into the habit of not working, you become less and less likely, as the months go on, to want to return to your old job. And if you can find an opportunity to do something more pleasant or more lucrative on the side, while still collecting workers' compensation, human nature being what it is, it seems to be how many of these cases develop and morph into fraud.

Adam: You talked earlier about employers crossing the line in an effort to be competitive. Do you think they are crossing the line without realizing it, or do you think they are in denial?

Larry: I think denial has a lot to do with it. When you are in business you are in a competitive environment, and any edge that you can get seems to be legitimate or appropriate. You're trying to sell more of your product; you're trying to attract customers. If you can have a competitive edge in terms of pricing, that's going to help you sustain and grow your business. Because in a capitalist society you start out with that mind-set, it's very easy for that to morph over the line into fraud. And we find that that happens. And then people start to deny it. It's the same psychology that gets businesses jammed up with tax fraud. They're looking for that edge, they're looking to increase their profits, and they're looking to increase their competitiveness. There is also an attitude that "everyone else is doing it, and if I don't do it, I'm not going to be able to compete." Sometimes employers are forced into fraud by an overly hot competitive environment. Sometimes they feel that if they don't start cheating, like the guy down the block, their business is going to suffer.

So, yes, fraud seems to generate more fraud. Fraud seems to push otherwise legitimate people over the line, to kind of join the pack in order to survive. I once had a business owner come to me and describe precisely that situation. His concern was that he had a competitor in his business that was able to undercut him by using a number of tactics. First, the competitor used off-the-books labor and did not pay union scales to the off-the-books labor. Second, as part of that, of course, the competitor did not pay the appropriate share of withholding taxes. Third, the competitor's workers' compensation premium did not reflect that payroll.

By doing that, the competitor was able to under-price the gentleman I was talking with. And his attitude was, "I want to stay in business, I want to thrive. A lot of families depend on me. If you can't drive fraud out of my industry, how can I survive without just joining the party?"

Adam: How big is that "party"?

Larry: That's really, really hard to estimate. There is not much hard academic research on this issue, but there was one good study done several years ago in California that indicated that in California, during the last recession, payroll in the construction industry was being underreported to the carriers by as much as 70 percent.

Adam: What percentage of claims do you think are fraudulent?

Larry: It's definitely a minority. It's my opinion that the majority of the claims start out legitimate and that the majority of claims stay legitimate.

Adam: What's interesting is that employers feel most claims are fraudulent.

Larry: I've encountered that, and I understand where it comes from, but I don't agree with it. A lot of it is simple frustration. They're basically paying out for somebody who is not working, and either the rest of the workforce has to pick up the slack or they have to hire somebody else. They don't understand why this person isn't returning to work. Just because the person isn't returning to work doesn't mean the person is engaging in criminal fraud. The person may be abusing the system by staying out longer than an employer would like, but that's not fraud; that's abuse.

Adam: Do you find fraudulent claims with $20,000 of medical expenses?

Larry: Sure, there are a number of ways you can find even higher medical expenses and fraud. One of the interactions that you see is the interaction between the fraudulent claim and the abuse of prescription drugs, especially narcotics. Sometimes a fraudulent claim is also a claim that involves a claimant who was or became addicted to pain killers, and the claim is a continuing source of pain killers for them. So sure, that can happen, and does happen. Sometimes the doctors may even be complicit in this. But, in most cases, pain is a subjective thing, and the doctor will tend to accept and will prescribe appropriately to what the patient describes as his or her level of pain. But if the claimant is lying about how much pain he or she is in, the claimant can usually get some heavy-duty narcotics.

Adam: If employers suspect fraud, what should they do?

Larry: If employers suspect fraud, they are already three steps behind. What they should do needs to start at the time of injury. The most important things that employers should do on every report of an injured worker is to have a form and a process for finding out what happened, to listen carefully and take seriously what the employee is saying at the time of injury, and to properly record it.

Adam: "Properly record" means what?

Larry: It means you should have an incident report that you use in every case of an injury and see that it is fully filled out by a supervisor, based on that interview with the employee as soon as that's possible to do. If you don't do that and you wait until the time that the claim is actually filed, that may be a couple of weeks later, or even further down the road, and the story may have already morphed once or twice. So as close to the time of injury that you can, get an accurate statement of what happened, and that includes talking to any workers who may have witnessed it, and it includes isolating any tapes from surveillance cameras you may have on your premises and saving them. That's the first step you should be taking, even before you suspect any fraud in a claim, so that later on down the road, you have those things locked in, and that gives the carrier or the carrier's investigators a place to work.

But, getting back to the question, when you get to the point that you suspect fraud, the first thing you need to do is talk to the carrier's claim department, and you need to articulate why you think it's fraud. And from there, the carrier should be able to pick up on it and decide if the concern is legitimate and should be further investigated. But again, not every abuse is fraud. Not every claim of abuse should be investigated by the special investigations unit. It's important that employers know what is and is not fraud and understand what kind of response they are going to get from their carrier.

Adam: Are there certain red flags that employers should look for?

Larry: Sure. First of all, they should be thinking about what their relationship was with this worker. Was this one of the good guys, the guy who went the extra mile for you? The guy who came to work every day with a positive attitude? Or was this one of your problem children? Your problem children are more likely your candidates for a staged accident or for malingering.

Secondly, was there anything going on at work which might have triggered a false claim, such as a layoff, a disciplinary action, the firing of an individual worker just before the claim was filed? Those are important red flags. What fellow employees are saying with respect to the injured worker is also important. We've seen cases where employees have boasted to their peers that they were going to stage an accident and go out on workers' compensation. It may be common talk in your business, and you need to have an ear to the ground about that and be sensitive to it.

The next thing is, if you are big enough to have an HR department, has the HR department done outreach to the injured worker? Have you called as a follow-up within the first week just to check and see...do the human thing. How does she feel? How does he feel? Are you getting any better? Is there anything we can do for you? Many times keeping that connection with the injured worker will prevent fraud from occurring. Because, first of all, it shows some human decency; it shows some human concern. And, second, it shows that the employee hasn't fallen off your radar screen. When people start to feel invisible, there's more of a temptation for fraud. So, if you start picking those things up, those are indicators. Also, how long has this been dragging on? Has it been going on for six months, eight months? Have you offered the employee a return-to-work with light-duty and been refused despite a medical clearance? Did the employee change doctors because the employee didn't like getting a medical clearance to return to light-duty?

A lot of this is common sense. But if you're starting to see a pattern develop where that kind of behavior is taking place, you need to be concerned. If HR calls an injured worker at home and can't get the person on the phone during the day, well, that's a big red flag. Where is the employee? If they're too sick to come to work, well, then probably they should be spending a large amount of time at home, at the doctor's office, or in physical therapy. But you should be able to get them at home during the workday, and if you can't, that's a big red flag. Why not? Where are they? What are they doing? I'm not suggesting that the employer conduct a full-scale investigation, but if you've kept light contact with the employee, in a friendly concerned way, you can pick up a lot of information that will tell you that a claim is starting to go sour.

Adam: And what about the Monday morning claim, where someone may have been hurt playing touch football on Saturday?

Larry: Oh sure, but you're going to pick a lot of that up at the water cooler. A good employer, a good manager, a good foreman, a good supervisor knows enough about the staff to know who's a skier, who is a jet skier, who goes hunting. And they have a feel of what their staff intends to do next weekend. They won't pick up on all of it—I mean, you don't—but you'll pick up on enough to know that in many cases, your employee went skiing on Sunday. And Monday morning, if there's an accident, especially if it's an unwitnessed accident, or if it is an accident in an unusual part of the facility where that employee wouldn't be, that's a red flag; that's something to be concerned about. Could it be legitimate? Sure, but it is certainly something to be concerned about. And again, if there are surveillance tapes available in the facility, those should immediately be sequestered and looked at. You don't want to be overly suspicious, but you do have to be somewhat careful.

Adam: Is establishing a culture of caring the number one deterrent of fraud?

Larry: Absolutely, absolutely. When employees feel connected to their jobs, connected to the people they work for, and connected to their peers, I think the likelihood of fraud decreases drastically.

Adam: Is there anything else employers can do to fight fraud?

Larry: Employers need to understand the limitations that the carriers have. One of the limitations that we have is that investigative resources are expensive. Ultimately, the employers, who pay for the insurance, pay for the use of those resources. The carriers want to use them carefully, and we don't want to waste them just because an employer feels frustrated. Fraud involves an intentional lie in writing. If there is no intentional lie in writing, there is no fraud, even if the person is healthy enough to be back to work. No lie, no fraud. That's just the way the law works. If we don't have written lies in place that we can prove are lies, it's a waste of time and money to do surveillance.

Adam: Do you have any interesting stories that you want to share?

Larry: Oh sure, they're all "you can't make this stuff up" stories. We had a case a number of years ago involving a registered nurse who went out with a back problem. We got wind of the fact that she was advertising in somewhat seedy publications that she was a masseuse. And, in fact, she was offering more than massages. We have a videotape of her giving a back massage to an undercover investigator, in which she admitted that she was making more money in her new profession than she ever made as a registered nurse. Bingo, I've got a case right there, because she's admitting to making more money than she would ever be permitted to make with benefits. We had a case involving a person who was out on compensation, who relocated to Florida and got a job running a car dealership. The person was making close to six figures in their new job and collecting four hundred dollars a week at the same time on workers' compensation. That stands out because it's just pure greed. The person didn't need the money, but felt safe in continuing to steal it.

Adam: How often do you find doctors are conspirators in fraud?

Larry: Seldom. Most doctors are legitimate. They are legitimately trying to deal with patients' needs based upon the objective symptoms they find. Since so much of what they deal with is based on the patient's report, they may become unwitting cooperators in fraud because they have no choice but to rely on the patient when the patient says this is where it hurts and it hurts this much.

Adam: In group medical insurance there is accountability and transparency because the patient sees the bills?

Larry: Yes.

Adam: Would copying claimants and employers on medical billings reduce medical fraud overbilling?

Larry: An explanation of benefits going to claimants, I think is an excellent idea on a number of levels, but it's not without problems. Number one, it educates all employees as to exactly how much is being paid on their behalf. I think most comp. claimants have absolutely no idea about how much is being paid out for their medical care and probably would be shocked if they knew and probably would be appreciative if they knew. Second, claimants are the people who know what was done for them by health-care providers, and some of them are not shy about contradicting a doctor's bill. Knowing that an explanation of benefits went to the claimants would act as a deterrent to false billing by the small minority of doctors who maybe engaged in it. There's a problem with it, and the problem is the same thing people find when they look at what they get from their medical insurance: it's reading and under-standing explanations of benefits because it's not in plain English. You've got treatment codes, and you've got descriptions of treatment codes, and many times they don't make much sense to a layperson. In order to get the maximum effect from that kind of a program, one would need to do a plain English translation of the medical billing codes.

Adam: Are doctors and attorneys more difficult to pros-ecute than claimants and employers?

Larry: Sure. Anybody who can afford to employ the best attorney, and has a license at stake as motivation, is going to be more difficult to prosecute. They are also going to be less likely to make stupid mistakes in the first place and be easily caught. That's just a fact of life. That being said, I've had successes with prosecuting professionals. It can be done, and they shouldn't get a pass just because it's tougher to prosecute them.

Adam: What type of fraud have you had success in prosecuting?

Larry: Usually we have success with providers. Success comes because when you look at the whole gamut of their billing overtime, you start to see patterns of overcharging. Either that or you have claimants who will come in and tell you, "I did not receive this treatment." From there, many law enforcement agencies will do undercover work, where they send detectives and other operatives in to receive treatment from a healthcare professional. Then we take a look at the billing.

Adam: How did the claimant know there was a bill for services not rendered?

Larry: Because a sharp claims person in the insurance company had a conversation with the claimant on other issues and just happened to casually ask, "I see that you have been seeing Dr. X, and how's your treatment going?" And the claimant said, "What are you talking about? I haven't seen Dr. X in two years." The bills kept coming in.

Adam: Has social media been helpful in prosecuting fraud?

Larry: I think that has been overblown in terms of its impact. It's an intriguing concept. To really use social media, you would have to engage in a level of intrusiveness that goes beyond just reading the person's public Facebook or MySpace page. You have to friend that person on a pretext, you have to get past that front page they show the whole world.

Adam: Do you think fraud will be more difficult to get away with as technology improves?

Larry: It's not so much that technology needs to improve. Our ability to investigate and prosecute fraud will get better when we get better at accessing and correlating the massive amounts of data that already exist. Like it or not, we live in a society where massive amounts of information are kept in various places on all of us, and to some degree, the systems talk more to each other than they used to. But we've also, for very legitimate reasons, put up a lot of firewalls between various systems that do impede the ability to gather information and to do an effective investigation. For example, we have tax secrecy laws which not only have legitimate purposes but also impede our ability to get at what a business might actually be engaged in. There are many ways we put information in boxes, where, if we had easier ways of accessing these boxes, we would be much more effective. But that all comes at a cost; it comes at a cost of privacy. And as a society, we have to decide how; sometimes it's better not to allow investigators to be too effective because the price we pay in terms of privacy is too high. Even if it means some bad guys don't get caught.

Adam: Larry, what did you like most about your career?

Larry: What I enjoyed the most about my career, both in insurance and in tax, was that every day was a new challenge. You really got to see the inventiveness of the human mind as you see all the different ways that people find to game the various systems. We used to say that if people spent half the energy that they devote to cheating you out of $50 to making money legitimately, they could make five times the amount of what they cheated you out of.

Adam: What drives your effort to pursue fraud?

Larry: It's a game, in a sense. There's some satisfaction about catching people who cheat. Cheating offends my moral sense, as it does most people. But it's a puzzle. Sometimes I feel like Dr. Gregory House, on television. The puzzle is, and can be, very fascinating.

Adam: How has exposure to so much fraud had an impact on you personally?

Larry: It makes me be more and more careful in my personal life to understand where the lines are and not to cross them.

Adam: What improvements would you like to see in the system to make anti-fraud efforts more effective?

Larry: Again, speaking personally, I would like to see the Workers' Compensation Board undertake a serious analysis of their practices and procedures to determine how they could be more fraud resistant. The goals of the workers' compensation system are worthy and appropriate. Injured workers need to be protected, that is goal number one, and it always has to be goal number one. However, one of the priorities for the Board increasingly needs to be making sure that the system becomes more resistant to being gamed by the various players who will game it.

Adam: What achievements are you most proud of?

Larry: Oh, that's a hard question. I'm most proud of having had the opportunity during my tenure at the State Fund of assembling an outstanding team of investigators who really do get it and are motivated to do full and fair investigations, to call it like they see it. That involves a lot. It involves saying, "Yes, there's a case here," but it also involves the courage to say, "No, there's no case…we can't do anything with this; let it go." Sometimes, you get a lot of pressure not to do that. One of my jobs that I'm proud of is that I've always backed my staff when they've said to me, "No, we have to let this one go." It's a serious matter to accuse somebody of a crime. You want to make sure that if you're going to do that, you'd better be right.

Adam: What was your biggest frustration in fighting fraud?

Larry: The amount of time it took before people started to take, not just workers' compensation fraud but also insurance fraud and tax fraud, to get them to take it more seriously. Our society is changing; our culture is changing. We are not the people our grand-parents were, unfortunately, in many respects. I think we are more selfish than they were, and because we are more selfish than they were, I think that more people are inclined to do dishonest things. That saddens me. That frustrates me, but we need to take it seriously and take real efforts to minimize fraud.

Adam: Do you think that we are winning the battle?

Larry: I think we're starting to win. It's a long struggle. You have to keep your eyes on the ball. Every four years we elect a new executive in the state. Every two years we elect a new legislator. Every four years we elect new pros-ecutors and new judges, periodically. So education has to be ongoing to keep fraud on the radar of the people who we elect to take care of these issues.

Adam: If you could start your career in prosecuting fraud over again, what would you do differently?

Larry: (Laughs) I don't know, probably not very much. I wish that when I was assistant district attorney, I had taken white-collar crime more seriously. And I wish that I had the opportunity to work more in the insur-ance industry at the beginning of my career, rather than in the middle and later years of it, because it is a fasci-nating industry. I also wish that we had more resources to fight white-collar crime throughout my career. It's really hard to get that kind of commitment, especially in tough economic times, to doing that kind of thing. But yes, I wish I'd known more about the insurance industry early in my career and when I was a prosecutor.

Adam: Is there anything you would like to add?

Larry: Yes, I touched on it earlier. Since we are talking a lot about employers and what they need to do, they need to understand very clearly that if they don't understand that abuse and fraud are different, they're going to be very frustrated. Abuse and fraud are different problems. If an employer believes that every time an employee takes too long to come back to work, it's fraud and that the employee should be locked up, the employer is just plain wrong. That's not how the system was set up, and that's not how you need to address that problem. If you need to get an employee back to work, you need to take care of that with the employee by the culture you establish and by the follow-up you do that shows you want the employee back.

Adam: Thank you, Larry.

Chapter 6

Interview with Ed Hiller, Director of Claims and Medical Operations, NYSIF

Mr. Edward L. Hiller is the director of Claims and Medical Operations for the New York State Insurance Fund (NYSIF), New York's largest workers' compensation insurer. He has been serving in that capacity since January 2000.

During his tenure as claims director for NYSIF, Mr. Hiller has been instrumental in leading the Fund's conversion to an electronic, paperless claims environment.

Mr. Hiller joined NYSIF in 1982 as an attorney trainee in the Legal Department, Third-Party Division. He worked his way up to the title of principal attorney. He served as the head of the Legal Department's Litigation Division under two general attorneys. In that capacity, Mr. Hiller was responsible for the defense of NYSIF's policyholders in schedule 1B unlimited exposure court-house lawsuits, also known as *Dole v. Dow* cases.

Mr. Hiller holds a bachelor of arts degree from the University of Albany and is a graduate of Brooklyn Law School, where he was a member of the Moot Court Honor Society. Before joining NYSIF, he engaged in international underwriting in the excess and surplus market.

He is a member of the New York State Bar Association, American Association of State Compensation Insurance Funds (AASCIF), the American Society of Workers' Comp. Professionals, Inc. (AMCOMP), and the New York Claims Association (NYCA), of which he is a past president. He is admitted to the practice of law in New York and New Jersey as well as in the United States District Courts for the Southern and Eastern Districts of New York. In 2003, Mr. Hiller earned the designation Workers' Compensation Professional (WCP) from AMCOMP.

In December 2008, Mr. Hiller was honored by the NYCA at the Harvard Club of New York in recognition of excellence in service to the insurance industry.

Adam: Ed, thank you for participating.

Ed: Thank you. First, these are my opinions only, not necessarily the NYS Insurance Fund's (NYSIF).

Adam: I would like start with an overview of what reserves are and how they're established.

Ed: Great question. Probably one of the most important things that we do here is to set timely and accurate reserves. It's one of the foundations of good claims management. A reserve is the thought-out, best estimate that one can make, based on all the information available, as to what to expect to pay on a particular claim in the future, until the claim is resolved—both for compensation and for medical costs.

Adam: How accurate is the reserving process?

Ed: We've come a long way at NYSIF. The worst practice in the industry is what's known as step reserving. This is when the case manager will simply throw dollars on a case as needed. For example, if a medical bill comes in for $300, the case manager increases the medical reserve by $300. This kind of piecework is the worst possible way to manage a case. The reserve reflects the overall claim strategy on getting the case resolved at the earliest possible time.

Reserving is a combination of an art and a science. So, the most important thing, and probably will be a theme throughout what we're talking about today, is communication. We have to get communication from the claimant's side of the case as well as the employer's side and especially on the medical side. Once we know what the injuries are, and have taken into account the age and other health characteristics of the claimant, we've given our staff the tools that they need to set the reserves both for compensation and medical costs. We have a tool on our electronic claim file, which we call CHS, or Case Handling System, which lists injuries of various types. And based on information gathered by national consultants, we are able to get an estimate of how long the claimant should be treated, based on the injury; how long it should take for the claimant to return to work; and how much it should cost.

So if the injury is, let's say, a broken arm and the data is based on an otherwise healthy forty-year-old male, the consultant's data says the recovery time for that injury, let's say, is eight weeks, and the claimant's wages were $600 a week, so we know that the comp. will be two-thirds of that. And then we can extrapolate from that times twelve, so we have a compensation reserve or the basis for a compensation reserve. And the same thing with the medical reserve. They'll give us the dollar amount, the length, the duration, and the treatment. There will be the casting and the follow-up medical, and let's say, it's $5,200. That will be the basis for our medical reserve.

Adam: What is an IME, and what is its purpose?

Ed: An IME means an independent medical examination. It's a tool that a carrier would use in defending against a comp. case. Often workers' compensation cases will come down to a so-called battle of the doctors. There are claimants' doctors out there that will basically give a claimant whatever the claimant's attorney wants them to say. That's the hard reality of it. And we're allowed to bring in our own medical expert to get an independent view. Or our IME may verify what the claimant's treating physician found. We're not looking to beat anyone. We're trying to get to the truth. We not only want to treat the claimants fairly, but we also want to be treated fairly. So we will have the claimant go for an examination, and the doctor is mandated by statute to provide copies of the reports to all parties of interest in the case within a certain time frame. And then there will usually be a hearing, and the doctor may or may not testify. The report will come into evidence, and the law judge will render a decision.

Adam: Do you believe loss control is effective in preventing claims, and are employers fully utilizing and embracing this strategy?

Ed: We have a very active field services department that will go out and really try to empower the employers to maintain a safe, or safer, working environment. It's all about communication, and it's all about the attitude of the employer as well.

Adam: What do you mean by that?

Ed: There has to be buy-in by the policyholder. You can have the most wonderful early-return-to-work program, for example, on paper, with the glossiest brochures. But if the policyholder has the attitude that "This is why I have comp. insurance; I can't be bothered with this stuff," it won't be effective. There has to be buy-in on the part of the policyholder. If the policyholder makes a concerted effort to improve safety in the workplace, of course it can have a beneficial effect on claims.

Adam: How can employers enable hearing representatives to represent them better?

Ed: Well hearing representatives are, in effect, the counsel for the policyholder in the court, which in our case is the Workers' Compensation Board where administrative law judges preside. How can the hearing reps be helped by the policyholder? Again, it's the communication word. The employer has to keep us in the loop. The employer has to give us every bit of information that they know about the case. And the employer has to cooperate with us when we need the employer to fill out forms and to testify.

Adam: What techniques does NYSIF use to reduce the cost and life of a claim?

Ed: We preach a trinity here to our claims managers: Reserve. Strategy. Diary. The three legs of the stool. We discuss what reserves are—the financial blueprint for the case reflecting a well-thought-out strategy to get the claimant to the best possible medical improvement in order to return to work—that's always the key—at the earliest possible time. And the diary ensures that the case manager will follow up with the strategy and take the next step, whatever it may be, to get the case resolved. That's the prize. Reserve, strategy, and diary are our keys.

Adam: How have the 2007 New York reforms had an impact on the claims process?

Ed: In terms of the claims process itself, the day-to-day nitty-gritty workflow, I would say not greatly, but in terms of financials, they have had an extremely negative impact on our ability to manage cases within reasonable cost boundaries.

As you know, the claimants began getting their raises in 2007. So, at that time, the highest indemnity payment we would make on a weekly basis, regardless of how much the claimant was earning, was $400. It's gone up every year since then. It's now $740 a week, tax-free, and is now adjusted to the average weekly wage of all earners within the State of New York, including all of the extremely highly paid people. So, if the economy continues to improve, we're looking at the dawn of a new age of the $1,000-a-week tax-free claimant. And considering how difficult it is to get certain claimants to go back to work, even when they were making $400 a week, how are we going to get them to go back to work when they're sitting at home collecting $1,000 a week, tax-free? So, I think the picture is bleak right now, unless and until we can get the benefit of the bargain that was made in that legislation, which was an increase in the indemnity rate, which was long overdue—we'll concede that—in exchange for a cap on permanent partial disability cases, which we have seen honored only in the breach as we are still awaiting an adoption of the durational guidelines by the Workers' Compensation Board.

So, in effect, the claimants now have the best of both worlds. They're getting the increased amounts. There are no caps to speak of. Very few have we seen. And even if we do get a cap, the cap does not begin until the case is classified. So it doesn't relate back to the date of accident, which I think is a flaw in the legislation. The claimants' attorneys now have no incentive to get their cases classified. And we have seen, in a study that we did internally, a 90 percent drop-off in the number of classifications that we were getting pre-compensation reform. So the promised savings that were supposed to come out of that legislation have not transpired. In fact, the opposite is true. Costs are skyrocketing.

Adam: What does having a case "classified" mean?

Ed: Classified means that a Workers' Compensation law judge has decided that the person's permanently partially disabled or permanently totally disabled, which means, in the New York scheme with the albeit elusive caps, that these claimants get paid for the rest of their lives.

Adam: What did you mean by the cap on permanent partial disability has been "honored only in the breach"?

Ed: In other words, even though the Board has not adopted disability durational guidelines, the Board has instructed its judges, its law judges, that they still may, and should, impose caps on cases when appropriate, using basically the standards that were in effect before the legislation, when they would say, "I find the claimant is permanently partially disabled," and could give a certain percentage of disability. And then there's a table within the statute that says how many weeks that would translate into compensation. Ten years is the maximum; that's for people who are 96 percent or more disabled. The judges know how to do it, but the judges all run their own show. They've all been instructed to do it, but only some are doing it.

Adam: What steps can the State Fund take to get them back to work?

Ed: We hope claimants are self-motivated to get back to work. If we have reason to believe a claimant is malingering, we can have an IME and bring in a doctor who might testify that the claimant is perfectly fine and able to return to work, and then we can ask for a hearing to stop our liability to continue payments.

Adam: Do you feel that the system is supportive, or are you fighting the system?

Ed: It's a claimant's system. It's a claimant's world. Just about every presumption in the law is in favor of the claimant, starting with the presumption of compensability. So even an unwitnessed accident can, of course, be compensable. The claimant says he was in a dark room, bent over, and hurt his back. And then he gets an MRI, and it shows two herniated disks. Whether or not it happened the way he says, it happened. In all likelihood, that case will be compensable. And a very high percentage of the adult population over the age of forty-five, studies have shown, will have some symptomatic result on a spinal X-ray, simply because of the aging process and the effects of gravity. So it's a claimant's world.

Adam: For claims that occurred after the 2007 reforms, what is the basis for establishing their reserves?

Ed: That's an excellent question. If we're certain, or nearly certain, that the case will eventually be classified, we try to reserve it as if there will be a cap, and we do our best to estimate it—as to what it will be eventually. And, as we've discussed, reserving is a fluid process, so the reserve is always subject to change. Once the case is finally capped, then we know, and then we have what insurers crave, which is certainty. Then we can fearlessly impose the cap on the reserve.

Adam: What improvements in the workers' compensation system are helping employers?

Ed: I think the Fund and the Board have made great strides in facilitating the electronic exchange of information. This adds efficiencies to the system.

Adam: Where are you seeing ongoing difficulties in the workers' compensation system?

Ed: We'd like to see, and I think the claimants would agree, faster turnaround times between hearings and decisions and faster scheduled hearings. I know the Board is trying to work on that. More efficiency in the system, perhaps fewer hearings. I know the Board is trying to work on that. More expedited decisions. And we'd like to settle more cases as well.

Adam: What should employers be doing to reduce the cost of claims?

Ed: Communicate with us. Give us everything we need to know about the case. Show up for hearings. Fill out the forms we ask you to fill out. And reach out to employees who are injured. Let them know that they're important to you and you want them back to work, but that you can't hold their jobs forever.

Adam: Is there evidence to prove that return-to-work programs help employers?

Ed: I think, of course, there's evidence to support that active return-to-work programs, where there's full employer buy-in, are more efficient than those where employers take a laissez-faire approach.

Adam: Do you think establishing a culture of caring about safety is the most effective claims reduction strategy?

Ed: Of course that's important. It seems like basic common sense. But not only do they have to talk the talk; they also have to walk the walk. All that talk in the world is useless if they don't have the first-aid kit on the premises.

Adam: In 2009, NYSIF insured 41 percent of the New York market. Does NYSIF offer advantages to employers due to their scale and size?

Ed: Well, I'm prejudiced, but I think absolutely yes. What we offer more than anything else is an incomparable compilation of human knowledge and experience. The State Fund is like one big extended family. And we have employees here with an incredible amount of longevity and experience. Someone at State Fund, Adam, with twenty years' experience is like a rookie compared to some other companies. People have and are still making careers here. It's kind of old-fashioned.

Just in my little group alone, my inner circle, so to speak, I have twenty-eight years of experience, and I'm not even close to being the most senior person in terms of seniority. Thirty years' experience. Thirty-five years' experience. People who have run really the gamut, have done everything there is to do in a claims operation. Many started out as case managers, became hearing reps, became supervisors, became unit heads, and became heads of their own district offices. And we also have our own extraordinarily talented and cooperative ITS (information technology specialists) who have become, themselves, claims experts.

Adam: Do proactive employers who stay in touch with injured workers have better results?

Ed: Certainly. In fact, we have one employer, it's a large hospital, which actually brings its injured workers in, something like, I think, once a week, to see how they are doing and remind them, "Time is a wasting; let's get you back here as soon as you're able to."

Adam: If an employer has a "questionable" claim, what would you advise?

Ed: Communicate and tell us why. The system has become more cumbersome for us to controvert cases, with penalties for frivolous controversies. So we can no longer file what used to be known in the trade as the Protective C-7. We have to have a substantive reason, or reasons, and so state in the form, in advance of the hearing, as to why we feel the case is suspect and not compensable. And the employer is going to be, almost invariably, the best source of information for that.

Adam: When is it too late for an employer or carrier to contest a claim?

Ed: A form C-7 Notice of Controversy must be filed on or before the eighteenth day of disability, within ten days after the employer learns of the alleged accident, or within twenty-five days after notice of indexing by the Board.

Adam: What is the process that NYSIF follows when made aware of a possibly fraudulent claim?

Ed: We investigate. We reach out to the employer, and we take other steps as we deem necessary, which may or may not include using one of our outside vendors to conduct surveillance.

Adam: What can employers do to improve screening when hiring employees?

Ed: I think that they should do a thorough background check, and they should do drug testing. I think that it would be something that would pay large dividends in the future without buying themselves into big problems in the present.

Adam: How does early return to work reduce the size of claims?

Ed: Well, once a claimant returns to work, we're not liable for paying them lost wages anymore, which is, in New York, by far the biggest cost driver. About 75 percent of the approximately $1 billion we pay out in compensation and medical costs in a given year is for compensation. In terms of the numbers, the medical costs are a relatively small piece. So always the prize, always the goal, is to get the claimants healthy and back to work. Get the case retired.

Adam: I've seen a claim reserved for $50,000, increase to $250,000. What accounts for that?

Ed: Even if it's being handled properly, it's possible that could happen. That's why it's always a fluid process and we don't want to step reserve. We want to base our reserves on information. So if a case is initially reserved for $50,000 and you see it increased to $250,000, that should mean that we have learned something we didn't know before. For example, maybe a claimant who started out with a scratched toe has now developed reflex sympathetic dystrophy (RDS), where the body starts to rebel against itself. This happens. RDS is a condition that's problematical in comp. and medical costs. Or we'll learn that an orthopedic-type injury that we thought could be treated with bed rest and heat is going to turn out to need major surgery, a knee replacement or a hip replacement. You could see that the surgery bills would be very high.

Adam: Do you see these large escalations from back injuries?

Ed: The back is, by far, the most common part of the body that we see as an injury. The back cases aren't usually catastrophic cases, but they are usually cases that can lead to classification. Unfortunately, we see some truly catastrophic cases involving paralysis and burns. And we treat those cases with special attention.

Adam: What types of claims do your registered nurses get involved with?

Ed: We're blessed to have over sixty registered nurses on staff throughout the state, and they provide a variety of great benefits to NYSIF. They're licensed medical professionals, so they bring true medical expertise. They get involved in discharge planning, utilization review, and some of them handle their own small caseload of actual claims, from cradle to the grave, where they do everything that's needed to be done on the case. That will usually be done in cases in which there are extremely serious injuries that require a lot of medical expertise. They also serve as in-house resources for the lay claim staff.

Adam: What is on your wish list to improve the workers' compensation system?

Ed: Get the cap on permanent partial disabilities going, please; that's the number one thing on my wish list, and to just kind of ease up on all the new changes that have been going on. The Workers' Compensation Board, I'm sure, means well. But everything that it decrees requires us to stop whatever we'd like to be doing and do what we have to be doing because that's the equivalent of what's called "statutory mandate." And everything that the Board changes requires programming on our part. And programming is not easy, and it's very time consuming. I would say take a deep breath. The system was not so horribly broken before. Give us the benefit of the bargain, and let us go about our business in an efficient way.

Adam: Why is there a gap between the reforms and the implementation of the caps on permanent partial disabilities?

Ed: It's not being implemented. The gap is the judges don't have what they feel is the necessary tool. They don't feel that they have been given the guidelines with which to invoke the number of weeks at which the claim should be capped. There is a draft out there now (November 2010) for the long-awaited durational guidelines, but it's still in the comments stage.

Adam: What's on your wish list with respect to employers?

Ed: Communicate with us, cooperate with us, and maintain the best possible safety program in the workplace. Always make safety the number one priority for you as a boss. And take advantage of our field services people. They do a great job.

Adam: What has been most memorable for you in your career?

Ed: I think probably, when I leave here, the one particular thing I'll remember most is what happened on September 11. Where I was sitting here at this desk, seven blocks north of Ground Zero, heard the first plane screeching overhead, heard the explosion into the first tower, looked out my window, and saw the black hole and the fire. Our people saw everything that day. I'll always remember how lucky we were that no one from the State Fund family was killed that day. I'll remember how people were calm and collected that day; how everyone stood together and supported each other; and how in the immediate aftermath of that day, the State Fund was able to keep functioning and didn't make a single late compensation payment, because we had gone to a paperless environment just a few months before 9/11. We were able to have our brothers and sisters in the other offices, not located here near Ground Zero, pick up the slack for us and adopt, so to speak, the New York

City claims, which comprise half of our claims statewide. Put some of these claims on extended payments. And we didn't even have a backlog of medical bills. Everyone pulled together. And then, two weeks later, when we allowed most of the staff to come back into the building, how our executive director was there greeting each person individually, comforting them, and how counseling was made available. And just how lucky we were and how everyone came together in the aftermath.

Adam: What do you like most about what you do?

Ed: What I like most about what I do is being privileged to spend time and to learn and work together with some of the most dedicated, intelligent, and knowledgeable people in the industry on a daily basis, our own State Fund people. And I especially enjoy going around and visiting the various business offices that we have throughout the state and getting to see the people that work in the districts.

Adam: Thank you, Ed.

Chapter 7

Interview with Brian Mittman, Claimants' Attorney

Brian Mittman is the managing partner of Markhoff & Mittman, PC, a law firm helping injured workers and their families since 1933. His practice focuses on workers' compensation claims, social security disability claims, and other disability-related matters. He is the author of *5 Deadly Sins That Can Derail Your New York Workers' Compensation Case*, a book he wrote to provide injured workers with the information they will need to help them understand their rights and the obstacles they face when dealing with insurance companies, the Workers' Compensation Board, and their employers.

Currently, Mr. Mittman serves as co-chair of the New York Workers' Compensation Alliance, as an executive board member of the Society of New York Workers' Compensation Bar Association, Inc., and is on the board for the Injured Workers' Bar Association, where he is the regional director for Westchester County. He is also on the board of directors for the White Plains Bar Association. As part of these responsibilities, Brian frequently makes presentations and writes articles for numerous publications in the industry. Brian is also a faculty member with Lawline.com, an online continuing education company for lawyers.

Adam: Brian, thank you. Can you please describe what you do?

Brian: Well, I have a disability law practice, and our main area of focus is New York State workers' compensation and social security disability, representing mostly injured workers.

Adam: Why do claimants hire you?

Brian: Claimants will hire me if they have been injured on the job and they are now going through the New York State workers' compensation system. Either they don't believe they are getting the benefits that they want or the bureaucracy is too intimidating or something may have happened with an insurance company or an employer and they believe they need help.

Adam: Why do you think they should hire you?

Brian: Well, that's a good question. The main reason why I think that they should hire an attorney is that it is really a bureaucratic swamp, a real nightmare in terms of trying to navigate the system of benefits. Not every claimant actually needs to have an attorney, but there are quite a lot of cases where people need to make sure that they get the right amount of weekly benefit and the right medical care and that they end their case the right way.

Adam: Do you think that an adversarial culture at work leads to employee retaliation?

Brian: I definitely think that an employer's business culture can affect if, when, and how someone files a claim. Over the years, I've seen companies that are very forthright with their employees, helping them out, getting the claims filed, and getting them back to work as soon as possible. I've seen other situations where there are very legitimate accidents and injured workers are stonewalled. I've also seen situations where it may not be very clear whether the injury is legitimate. So, culture and how people handle the claims definitely affect cases.

Adam: Do claimants with accommodating employers hire you anyway?

Brian: That's the type of case that will depend upon the injury. If, in New York, you have an injury to an extremity, you may be entitled to benefits at the end of the case, so I always encourage people to return to work because the benefit at the end will be a lot better. That really has nothing to do with the employer; it has to do with the actual law—making sure the medical reports are in order and dealing with the insurance company—so that's the type of case we would love to see. There might be other cases where someone is out of work for six weeks due to a back injury: the person goes back to work; no need for an attorney.

Adam: Are employees with legitimate claims who are not accommodated by their employer where you see most of your cases?

Brian: That's where we see a lot of the contention. We'll see people who have worked for years for a company get hurt through no fault of their own. Then, for some reason, either the employer's human resources department or a supervisor who might have a bad relationship with the injured worker, just doesn't want to help the worker out, report the claim, or file it the right way because of possible worries about premiums or something like that. I don't even know why [employers] are worried half the time. They bought the insurance. And then, all of a sudden, you have an injured worker who can't get benefits. And studies show that if somebody gets medical care, the sooner they get the medical care and they're taken care of, usually the quicker they'll get back to work.

Adam: Does a lawyer's involvement increase the cost of a claim?

Brian: I actually think a plaintiff claimant lawyer's involvement helps move cases along. I've seen far too many instances where defense costs, particularly in the New York State workers' compensation system, really drive a lot of costs and not necessarily for legitimate reasons. Attorney's fees for injured workers come out of the benefit the injured worker receives. It is not above and beyond the claim.

Adam: If you succeed in maximizing the benefits paid to your claimants, doesn't that increase the size of the claim?

Brian: Absolutely. It could increase the claim, but the law of social legislation is almost one hundred years old now. And it was designed to provide a weekly benefit and medical care to an injured worker. And in exchange for that, workers gave up the right to sue their employer. Employers know that they have to pay for an insurance policy and that they won't get sued. And the employees know if they get hurt, through no fault of their own, or even sometimes through their own fault, that they will get these benefits and they can get back to work. So, in a sense, the law is supposed to, and is designed to, lean that way. And there is a maximum amount you can get on a case, period. And with the changes in New York in

2007, almost all cases now will have a conclusion date, for at least what we call our indemnity or lost-wages benefits. So yes, a claimant's attorney will maximize that amount, but that's built into the system. Medical costs, I will agree, are definitely out of control for so many various reasons, but we have no control over that, other than trying to get the medical care that our client needs. So, yes, an award to a represented worker may be greater than an unrepresented worker, but is that really fair?

Adam: Is an unrepresented claimant at a disadvantage?

Brian: Fifteen years ago, I think an unrepresented claimant would have been at less of a disadvantage than now. The referees are law judges who watch these cases, and the Workers' Compensation Board, always a very paternalistic institution, tried to watch out for injured workers and leaned or favored them. And if somebody wasn't represented, a judge would walk the person through whatever the issues were, provide them with a hearing, and let them know whether to get an attorney or not. Within the last fifteen years, and particularly within the last four or five years, it has become an administrative disaster to the point that, even as attorneys, we have problems dealing with the Workers' Comp. Board, with insurance companies, and with the various case law that comes down. Instead of this being a fairly simple system in which an injured worker can get medical care and some benefits, it's become a long, drawn-out process.

Adam: Without representation, do you feel that claimants don't receive full benefits?

Brian: My personal opinion is, yes. I have cases all the time where someone comes to me with a legitimate injury and when I ask them about prior accidents, I'll find out that they might have broken a hand. It turns out the claimant was out of work for six weeks, received benefits, got a nice lengthy letter from the Workers' Compensation Board, explaining all their rights in very legalistic terms, but the claimant never did anything. That injured worker under the law is potentially entitled to the money for the permanent injury to the hand, aside from those six weeks of lost time. And I see that, more and more, people are showing up and they haven't gotten their full benefit from past injuries.

Adam: By full benefit, you mean a scheduled loss?

Brian: A scheduled loss, yes.

Adam: Why is it difficult to collect a scheduled loss?

Brian: This goes to what motivates or moves the case along. The Workers' Compensation Board today is very statistic-based. Once cases close, once they put certain values on the case, you'll receive a letter that says you've been paid this amount of money. If this is not correct, let us know; then there will be about a page and a half of pretty convoluted and complex language that explains that you might be entitled to an award for permanent injury in the future, if your doctor provides the report. A lot of people say, "Well I got paid while I was out; I got my medical care. All right, I'm back to work."

Adam: So they don't pursue it?

Brian: They don't pursue it.

Adam: What do you think employers should be doing to reduce claims and save money?

Brian: Well, this again goes all the way back to the purpose of the law. The idea was if the employer had to buy an insurance policy, the employer would be motivated to keep their workplace safe, or safer, but accidents happen. So, I think that employers certainly can make it clear and put into place what the procedures should be if you've been injured and the what, where, and how you should get medical care. The managers who deal with the employee should certainly be schooled in that issue. Employers need to be aware that there have to be certain clear procedures in place and they need to educate their workers about it. I don't think people are going to try to go out and get injured, particularly in this job market, just because they know they have workers' compensation. The benefits just don't pay enough to motivate somebody to stay out of work. I think that if there is a dispute, the employer has to immediately notify the insurance company. I see a lot of cases where people have been injured and the supervisor says, "Don't worry about it. Take some Advil; keep working," and that starts to compound the issue. If an employer sees that premiums are going up or that there are a lot of accidents, I think the answer isn't to blame the worker but to figure out what the heck is going on.

Adam: As an employer yourself, what additional steps might you take to avoid legal involvement?

Brian: That's actually a really good point, because as an employer myself, sometimes I cringe a little bit at my premium bill or when somebody does get hurt. There's kind of a knee-jerk reaction when I'm wearing my employer hat. Yet, at the same time, here I am representing injured workers. Again, I think the most important thing is to make sure that you have the insurance set in place and a procedure to say to an employee, "If you are hurt or injured, you need to report it. I want it in writing; here is a form that we use. We won't retaliate against you, and here is the insurance information." And at that point, your legal involvement should be over. The insurance company will contact you. They will need payroll information, and, if the person is back to work, information as to whether there is some type of light-duty position or alternate job you can provide the person. And that's important to think about because you have a business to run and still go forward. I know in the restaurant business, fortunately or unfortunately, depending on where you stand, there are a lot of undocumented workers. However, your alien status in New York does not matter, and if you're working, you're working, and if you're injured, you're injured. So even if you are circumventing certain issues and tax issues, you should still have a clear procedure in place.

Adam: What mistakes do you see employers make with their workers' comp?

Brian: A whole bunch of different mistakes. One is classification. You have a lot of employers using the term *misclassified* these days, where they'll try to finagle whether a person is an employee or an independent contractor, or they might class somebody as a factory floor worker instead of a management worker. That helps to save on premiums on the front side but kind of screws things up down the road.

Adam: How so?

Brian: Well, it depends on the insurance companies and the employers. Let's take the employer who believes a person is an independent contractor, but in the eyes of the law, that person is really an employee. Then we have to actually fight and litigate that case. That employer has paid a lower premium and now has issues with premiums and the insurance company. We've spent months and months fighting a case where a person should have gotten the treatment and benefits earlier and may have gotten back to work sooner. It compounds the problem. We have employers that just don't respond to insurance companies. Even if the guy is being paid off the books, give him a payroll of somebody that is paid on the books who is similar, and we're done. You're not getting into trouble. A lot of people will go back to work too soon and, because of their injuries, can't leave work early for therapy, then end up getting fired because they are "not performing their job." That can lead to issues outside of workers' compensation such as discrimination claims or wrongful termination.

Adam: Do you see that often?

Brian: I'm seeing it more and more.

Adam: Are employers acting in ways that are self-defeating?

Brian: Well, I think from an employer's perspective, it comes down to a question of respect. You don't have to be liked, and you probably don't want to be liked by everyone. But what is the culture where you are working? If an employee gets hurt, and I've heard complaints like, "They treat me like garbage"; "I got hurt on their job, and I gave them everything." That probably affects other people in the ranks and affects relationships between employees and management. But again, coming back to the culture, I really do think that there is an effect there. I have seen employers and employees who get along very well and it looks like the employee may not be coming back and the employer can't afford to keep paying a salary or can't provide a light-duty position. When they've worked together, everyone has gotten out of it fairly calmly. Whereas there are other times where some people want to fight with the employer or the employer wants to get rid of the employee, and there is just contention there.

Adam: What is the law with respect to termination of the employment of claimants?

Brian: In New York, you can be terminated if you are out on workers' compensation. It's not necessarily discrimination. New York is an employment at will state. You can basically be fired for any reason as long as it is not discriminatory. New York Workers' Compensation has a very specific discrimination section that says if you are terminated for trying to get workers' comp. benefits, then they basically have to bring you back. In all the years I've done it, I've never seen that successful. So, basically if you are working for me today, Adam, and you get hurt, I can say, "Here is the insurance information; here's the claim form." I file it, call the insurance company, and say, "This guy got hurt here; take care of him." I hang up the phone and say to you, "Oh, by the way, on your way out, clean out your desk, 'cause

I have to replace you," and since we don't have a contract, I can legitimately do that. Now you'll be angry; you'll think that I fired you because you got hurt, and that may be true, but how are you going to prove that? I can say, "Well, you know, you sounded like you'd be out of work for weeks and weeks, and I needed somebody in place." Now, the discrimination side could be if you're fifty years old and I already have a twenty-two-year-old in place to fill your spot and I'm paying that person a third of what I was paying you. You might be able to claim that you were actually fired for discrimination. But that's a separate issue from being injured while you are working.

Adam: Do claimants at home like being contacted by the employer?

Brian: Depends (laughs). I tend to try to avoid it because, unfortunately, I just don't think the parties really understand what's going on. I've seen employers try to set up injured workers. I've seen employees feel pressured to get back to work when they are not fully healthy and ready to do so. Some employers are good. They'll keep paying people while they are out of work. They'll encourage them to come back to work. They'll provide them with accommodations when they get back to work. And other employers might think you are completely sandbagging it and they are trying to find out what are you really doing. "What do you mean you are at home? You only hurt your back?" So, it can be a problem.

Adam: Do you hear disappointment from employees because they are not being contacted?

Brian: Yes, I hear that too, particularly from people who have been with somebody for a long time and have put a lot into the company. "Wow, I worked for this guy for so long, and I can't believe this. Can't believe they didn't contact me. Nobody visited me in the hospital. I didn't get any phone calls. I can't believe that they didn't even give me any insurance information." So there has to be somewhat of a balance. I'm not fully against the contact. But this goes back to putting into place a plan to say, "Hey, if a person gets injured, here's what we are going to do. Here's our little injury packet." And under the law they are required to give an injured worker this special packet that the Workers' Compensation Board has now created. But it really should be, "Hey, Adam, I'm so sorry you got hurt. Here is all the paperwork. Here's all the stuff. Here's your contact information. Our policy is that you have to speak to us once a week to let us know if you are able to come back or if we can accommodate for you." And if somebody does something like that, then, I think, the outcome is going to be a lot better. I actually compare it to what statistics have shown in medical malpractice cases. Statistics show that doctors who actually step forward, admit mistakes, and talk to their patients are sued so much less than doctors who just clam up.

Adam: Why do you think claimants commit fraud?

Brian: Oh, you had to ask me that question; I hoped you would ask me about employer fraud (laughs). I think that it depends on what we are talking about is fraud. Fraud implies intent: intent to defraud, intent to misconstrue facts, and to hide it from somebody to get something. There is a whole section of people who are accused of fraud, or have even sometimes been found to have committed workers' compensation fraud, who just may have made legitimate mistakes. "Oh, I didn't realize that what I was doing would be considered work, because I was volunteering at the church on Sunday." Or "I thought it would be OK because this is just a little side job I was doing." I tell people, "Look, if you make any type of money, do any type of work paid or unpaid, you have to let us know."

But then there is a group of people who think, "Let me do a little on the side, no big deal, and I'll still collect these benefits." They think that they'll get some benefit and money out of it. What's really pathetic is that most of the cases that you see, even those that I blog about sometimes on my Web site, are for very small amounts of money. A few thousand dollars here, a few thousand dollars there, and they're losing all their benefits; they may have been arrested. They may have to pay back fines. The crazy part is that a lot of times, the medical claim is legitimate. The doctors are confirming that there are legitimate injuries or problems. Yet, somebody played games and screwed things up. That is an unfortunate problem. Yet, I think that the statistics also show that now that New York State has been prosecuting fraud claims and employers for not having insurance or misclassifying payroll, they have recovered ten times as much money as they do against injured workers who are allegedly committing fraud.

Adam: Do you think there are systemic problems that encourage fraud?

Brian: Yeah, I think the systemic part is the fact that the law always lags behind reality. Particularly in this day and age, we all have our BlackBerrys, we're always connected. I had a very unfortunate case where a woman died. She had done about an hour's worth of work at home, was driving for forty minutes to the office to go to a meeting to talk about the work she was doing, and was killed during the drive. And that was found not to be covered because she was commuting to work. Where did work end, and where did work begin? We are always answering our BlackBerry. You're at your kids' soccer game and half the time you're answering something on you BlackBerry. Are you working or not working? The reality is that people are going to try to find a way to keep themselves busy and do something. Because somebody is disabled doesn't mean that he or she is an invalid who is sitting on a couch watching TV. What happens if you have somebody, a laborer, who is out of work for a bad back and they happen to have a knack for selling goods on eBay? Do they get penalized for that, particularly if they have been doing that while working as well? Actually, in the statute, there is a double standard there, because you can't consider the money that they made from eBay while they were working to determine their overall wages. Yet, if they are still doing that after they are injured, a lot of the court cases will consider those to be wages, and it becomes a problem.

Adam: Would they be arrested for that?

Brian: They could be. It is a real problem, and the law just hasn't caught up or adapted to how we live our lives these days.

Adam: Do you see claimants get depressed being out of work?

Brian: Absolutely, and that's one of the reasons why I encourage people to try to get themselves back to work in some respect. At a certain point, it becomes a downward spiral. I have an attorney, one of my partners, who has a bad back. And his back went out and I was like, "Yeah, yeah, yeah, OK, your back went out." I had been dealing with this for eighteen years. And he wanted me to bring him some files to the house. So I went over to his house, and when he answered the door, I had to look down. He had crawled to the door. Here he was for two weeks, and I'm saying to myself, "Wow, these are my clients." One minute, you can feel good, and another minute, you can feel bad. It can be a problem.

Adam: Why do you think employers think that almost every claim is fraudulent?

Brian: I think that a good piece of that is just modern culture. We've all been brainwashed so that when you say "fraud for workers' compensation," you think of the guy who got injured working, not of the employer committing multimillion-dollar fraud. "Oh well, how can it be legitimate? Everybody has a herniated or bulging disc; that's what the studies prove." So, we hear this over and over again. I try to call a spade, a spade. And I've lost cases where I tell people to go back to work and they don't want to, which is fine; they can go get another attorney. I think it is really a cultural issue.

It's also an issue of employers sometimes not wanting to face the realities of the business. There are places that are very unsafe, and the premiums go up. And a lot of those employers want to beat the increase by thinking that if the employees are all getting hurt, they are all full of it. And then there are legitimate stories, like these railroad employees out on the Long Island Rail Road who filed claims with the railroad retirement system.

It sounds a little odd that 95 percent of these guys are disabled. So you start to hear all of this stuff, and then your knee-jerk reaction is, "Is this legitimate?" We all have a mentality of "if you can't see it, you can't believe it" to a certain extent. If somebody breaks an arm, it's pretty easy to see it. If somebody really wrenches their back lifting something heavy and has a serious impingement that keeps them from walking properly, it's a little tougher to sometimes believe, particularly if the person seems pretty healthy but now, all of a sudden, is not.

Adam: Do medical providers play a role in fraud?

Brian: As of December 1, 2010, the medical treatment guideline will be in effect in New York. And these guidelines really spell out pretty strictly how a doctor is supposed to follow a treatment course, and if there is going to be any type of variance, what the doctor has to do to prove it is necessary. This is like anything else; there are mills out there, where they just turn cases, and it's wrong. And there are doctors out there who are excellent doctors, who are following a certain protocol on a certain belief. I would like to think that most of the doctors don't want to aid and abet fraud. There are definitely doctors out there who just are overwhelmed themselves and see a lot of patients. They don't want to hear somebody complaining, and they say, "Yeah, yeah, yeah. Fill out the form," check it off, and send it in. It can be an issue.

Adam: Do you think it's in the employer's interest to show up at hearings?

Brian: No, there is no reason for an employer to show up at a hearing. I don't think it helps or hurts in any way because if there is an insurance company representative there, then that's who the judge is going to pay attention to. That's who I'm going to deal with. The employer has no real say. Where it could help would be, again, with the communication issue. Most insurance companies don't really communicate with their insureds or their employers. I've had situations where I have gone in and the attorney says that the employer offered a light-duty job. My client says the employer never offered a light-duty job. Now I end up setting that case for trial, and we are going to bring the employer in to testify. If the employer had been at the hearing, they could have had their personnel folder and said, "Here is the day we offered [the claimant] a job." That can work, but it's kind of a pain to break somebody away from work for a few hours to go there.

Adam: Has a bad culture aggravated a claimant and they responded in a retaliatory way?

Brian: Yes, there are certainly instances when I've sensed that had the employer made a legitimate offer of light-duty work, it would have gotten the person back sooner. I can't say the person was malingering, but certainly, they may have been more motivated to have returned to work even with some pain, if the circumstances were set up properly. And to be honest, I'm sure there have been instances where the employer has been very accommodating for somebody who just hasn't wanted to go back for some reason or another.

Adam: Is there any area I have not asked you about that you would like to discuss?

Brian: I think that the injured workers are really better served if employers and workers understand what the system is supposed to be. I have the same little story every time someone comes in and I sign them up. "Workers' compensation is designed to pay you some kind of benefit while you are out, to get you medical care, and to try to get you back as soon as you are able to. I'm not your doctor, so you know your body and when you believe you are physically and mentally able to return to work; that's always the best course of action." And if employers and injured workers understand that, I think that would go far toward making it a lot better. People just have to understand that it is really about this whole culture idea. If your culture is "I want to give you a safe place to work," that's the key. And then if you get hurt, I want to try to help you get back on your feet. I think that it makes it far better for everybody.

Adam: Brian, thank you very much.

Chapter 8

Interview with Robert Firmbach, Loss Control and Safety Specialist

Mr. Robert P. Firmbach is the president of RPF Associates, an Occupational Safety and Health Administration (OSHA), Department of Transportation (DOT), safety and fire protection consulting company. In this capacity, he manages the company; provides technical assistance to clients; and develops safety, health, and property conservation programs for the industrial sector and for motor fleet and construction companies.

Prior to forming RPF Associates, Mr. Firmbach was the assistant vice president of Loss Control Service of AIG Risk Management, having started this division in 1978. Bob holds the AAS degree in fire safety, is a graduate of New York University's Center for Safety Education with studies in industrial and motor fleet accident prevention, and has more than forty years of experience in the safety field. He is a certified safety professional (CSP), an associate in risk management (ARM), and is licensed by the New York State Department of Labor as a workplace safety consultant (CSC).

Mr. Firmbach has also provided his clients with expert testimony for auto, construction, products, and retail store accident reconstruction. His other areas of expertise include construction, manufacturing, and printing.

Adam: Bob, what do you do?

Bob: I'm a safety consultant to both general industry and with New York Department of Environmental Protection. I write formal safety programs and then encourage clients to follow them. Generally, a safety program that I would use would consist of management taking an interest in safety and announcing it with a statement of policy. That's the number one thing that any safety program has to have—assigning someone the responsibility to oversee safety, to look at the accidents that have occurred, and to determine where they might occur in the future. If you continue along the same path, and you know what your accidents were but do nothing to eliminate their causes, chances are you're going to continue to have similar accidents in the future. Maybe you need to do better training. If you're having a problem with slip-and-fall accidents, why is that? Why are employees slipping? Is it the type of footwear that they're wearing? Or is it a floor issue, where you're cleaning the floors? I've seen where they've gone in warehouses with automatic cleaning machines. Boy, the machines get the floor spotless, but they also leave a trail of a wet surface and nobody's bothering to put up "Caution, wet floor" signs. So now you actually increase the potential for accidents by trying to clean something up. It's the law of unintended consequences. You need somebody who's in charge of safety who should answer directly to top management.

The other thing is to let the employees know that you care by telling them that you're interested in their safety and by putting up safety signs, safety materials, and banners. All those things can help. Make sure the safety committee does a thorough accident investigation. And a thorough accident investigation isn't, "Well, the guy was careless; he wasn't looking where he was walking, and he slipped on the grease on the floor." A true investigation is, "Why was the grease on the floor? Where did the grease come from?" Yeah, the unsafe act is the guy was carrying a tray of gauges and he didn't see the grease because the tray blocked his view or he probably wasn't paying attention. That's the unsafe act. The unsafe condition is the grease. Where did the grease come from? Well, maybe it came from the hi-lo machine that was leaking oil and nobody noticed. It's a chain of events, because no accident is just purely, "the guy wasn't paying attention, and he walked into the wall." It's very, very unlikely that that's the only reason. Maybe it was too dark to see that the wall was protruding out. Well, maybe we need better lighting in there; not just to tell the guy to be more careful. You need to teach the supervisors how to do an accident investigation the proper way.

Adam: What is the employee threshold for OSHA involvement?

Bob: They'll get involved when you have just one employee, but it's unlikely. A lot of people mistakenly believe that you have to have eleven or more employees. Under eleven employees, you don't have to fill out OSHA accident logs, and other record-keeping requirements are at a minimum, but you fall under OSHA the minute you hire one employee.

Adam: What motivates an employer to hire you?

Bob: I get brought in two or three different ways. Most of the time, it's not altruistic. It's not that a company wants to set up a safety program. It's usually because they're having too many accidents, and workers' compensation premium is going up, and their experience modification is going up tremendously—it's costing them money, or they got in trouble with OSHA. Or the company doesn't want to get in trouble with OSHA.

Adam: So, they're hiring you to save money or to avoid regulatory problems?

Bob: Which is also going to save them money.

Adam: With what kind of employer do you have the best success?

Bob: One that has top management involved in or reviewing what we set up, the safety committee, and follows up on what the safety director does. The best result is when the president or the chief of that division comes in with the safety committee and shows that he has an interest and that he's watching it. Then the committee will do something. If not, then it just becomes, "Well, yes, once a month we're going to have a meeting; and before the meeting I'll inspect my area; and when we're in the meeting, we'll discuss what accidents occurred; and we'll put it out to subcommittees to follow up on the investigation and so on and report back." That's what happens a lot of times.

Adam: How does a safety committee save employers money?

Bob: Well, if you have an effective safety committee that investigates accidents, and if you investigate unsafe acts that don't result in an injury, you have a much better chance of preventing an injury, which is the key to savings. You can go into a company and they only have three or four accidents a year, but they may have hundreds of incidents from unsafe acts. Near misses, we call them. And if you can get a culture going where you'll actually start to look at those, then you'll recognize that we have a problem in this area. Let's look at it, put two people from the committee on it, and have them report back to us next month. Let's find out what the problem is and get some recommendations. I want to know the most costly, the one in the middle that's not going to cost as much, and the least costly. And we will then take that to management. The safety committee is interested in preventing accidents through identifying hazards and unsafe acts that are out there, and eliminating them.

Adam: How would you build a culture of safety?

Bob: First thing I would do is a good analysis of all accidents going back as far as we can get documentation. Usually, you can look at the First Report of Injury, which is the C2 claims form. Get as much information off that as you can. Identify where the hazards are. And if the company doesn't have OSHA logs, they have to start to maintain them. You're required to maintain an annual list or a log of all reportable injuries, and then you're required to post that. But I would start with the questions, "What's the problem? Where are all our accidents coming from?" I always go back to that.

Adam: Isolate the problem?

Bob: Yes, what's our problem? Is our problem that the employees are not properly trained? Is it a language problem? Does management communicate to employees the importance of safety, or are they just told, "Get the job done. Just do it," until they get hurt.

Adam: Once they isolate the problem, what's the next step?

Bob: You can say, "I've got four different groups in my workforce. I have the people in the office, the warehouse, the truck drivers, and the machine shop." And you find out which group has the best accident record and take them to lunch to recognize their safety with a certificate for their team. Then the other groups think, "Well, that would be nice to have; maybe we can improve safety and be recognized." You get the people thinking and management shows that they care. You do it also by training the employees. Half an hour, even fifteen minutes, or you start to have your supervisors get everybody together once a week or once a month and hold a five-minute safety talk. We provide employees with these safety talks on various subjects. They've got to look at where the accidents are coming from. Do I have to do something about the various chemicals that they work with, or is it wearing personal protective equipment, such as wearing the right shoes and putting in a dress code, that says: "No one is allowed to work with sneakers." And in a lot of the places, employees come in with sandals, and you just can't have that.

Adam: Do employers recognize that their employees are their best asset and that safety maximizes results?

Bob: I've heard them say it, but it still comes down to the bottom line. All these people are very much bottom line oriented. I mean, they don't want their employees to get hurt, but when it comes to "That's got to get out the door," that's when all of that breaks down.

Adam: How do you help the employer stay focused on safety?

Bob: If you get the right information, like the experience modification, you say, "Look, here's your experience mod. at a 1.40. Do you realize that instead of $200,000, you're paying $280,000? You'll save $80,000 just by getting back to the manual rate through maintaining a focus on safety."

Adam: So you want a management that's involved in the process and a safety committee that's focused on their unsafe acts and conditions?

Bob: And that brings solutions to management, not problems. The biggest thing that I do with a safety committee is train the members to go to management and say, "There's a problem and here are three ways that we think you can solve the problem." You give him the option to pick something that we can do to try to prevent this from happening again. If a forklift operator runs over an employee's foot, well, do we need steel-toe shoes in there? Was she wearing sneakers? Someone was walking by a pallet, and the pallet was splintered, and the splinter went right in the side of the foot. Why? Well, because she was wearing cloth shoes? We recommend that you have a policy that everyone will come in wearing a sturdy work boot. If they're working in an area where there's a lot of moving machinery, or where they could drop things on their feet, maybe you need to have a safety shoe or a safety boot. A lot of things can be done with personal protective equipment. Companies offer protective equipment, but they don't enforce usage rules. A lot of times I do that through photographs. I go around taking pictures of feet, and then I say, "You're telling me that they're supposed to be wearing a work shoe, but here are twenty-five pictures of your people wearing sneakers." Also, I teach safety committees how to do their own inspection. I take the members on a walk, and I show them what is important to me.

Adam: Do employers need an outsourced partner to improve safety, or can it be done internally?

Bob: If employers have somebody who has some knowledge of safety, they can do it themselves. I've seen people who had no knowledge of safety, but who cared to learn about it, start to read the safety magazines, and attend a few training courses, become pretty good safety people. I tell safety committees that basic safety is common sense. If you walk into a room, you automatically know something's wrong there, because you're built that way. If you stand there long enough and look around, you'll start to pick out the unsafe conditions. You just don't do a "walk-through," you do a "walk-in" look at what's going on, and try to determine what the unsafe act or condition is. You're not going to get to the highly technical stuff necessarily.

Adam: What would be the highly technical stuff?

Bob: Machinery guarding, moving machinery, where a hand could get caught, or where a sleeve could get caught and it could be drawn in.

Adam: You are passionate about what you do.

Bob: I grew up in this business. I have forty-seven years in this business. This is the only thing I have ever done. I'm a safety professional. I feel that I can be effective, that I can make a difference. Unfortunately, most of the time—and I have one client right now that they had a death case—it's "get that job done," not necessarily get it done safely. It's got to be done safely.

Adam: Why don't employees wear protective goggles when needed?

Bob: They don't wear the goggles because the goggles are uncomfortable. They now have safety glasses. Guys tell me, "Well, I wear reading glasses." I say, "Fine, you can buy safety glasses with the cheaters built into them."

Adam: What are cheaters?

Bob: They are the reading glasses, and you can get them at different powers: .125, .150, .175, .200. They run about $45. But that's still not a whole lot of money for a guy to be protected, and that would be a regular glass with the bifocal in it, and then shields on the side. So he's got protection. If you don't need the glasses, then for $3 or $4, you buy these glasses that are ANSI (American National Standards Institute) approved. In other words, they meet the requirement as safety glasses, but you could wear these things to the beach. They're cool.

Adam: What shoes do you recommend for drivers on winter deliveries, and how do you get them to wear them?

Bob: Well, they don't necessarily need steel-toe safety shoes, but those little traction shoes, well, that becomes a matter of training with those guys. Somebody's got to meet with them and say, "Look guys, you have to assess your delivery situation. Now, you've got these things, and they're a little stronger than rubber bands. They'll go right on, and they'll go right over your boot. And if they don't fit right, we'll make sure that you get one that fits right, so it's not hard to get on and get off. If there's snow or ice, then put them on to make the delivery. When you get back to the truck, take them off. You don't have to wear them all the time. But don't try to walk on ice because you know you're going to slip and you're going to break your leg." And you have to try to motivate them: "If you're out, you're losing pay."

Adam: Basic safety may be common sense, but don't employers benefit from a loss-control expert to help them focus, create awareness, and guide them on how to run an effective safety committee without reinventing the wheel?

Bob: Yes. The same thing is true with safety glasses and nonskid attachment onto the boot. You can't just say, "Here it is." Same thing with a hard hat. Why do you have to wear the hard hat? A reasonable person, if you say why, will wear it. If I have a boiler guy, I don't give him a hard hat; I give him what they call a bump cap, because he's working down in areas where he's liable to bump up against a pipe as he lifts his head. And you say, "Here's how you use it. Here's why you use this instead of this big hat. Use the tools we're giving you to protect you."

Adam: Do you recommend back belts for lifting?
Bob: No.

Adam: Why?
Bob: Because it hasn't been proven that they do anything. They really don't do anything. If someone is trained properly on how to use the belt, then I say, OK, go ahead. The belt will do one thing: it will get your posture better. You get a guy with a belly, and if you put the belt on right, it's going to pull him in and it will kind of get his spine closer to its original S-curve. If he's got

a belly, you're not going to get it that close. But if he puts the belt on and leaves it on all day long, he's going to start to weaken his muscles. And when his muscles weaken, it's very easy for those muscles to rupture. And then he'll get hiatal hernias from wearing the belt too long, and his belly—unless he gets himself on a bit of a diet—is going to get even bigger.

Adam: With respect to retailers, do you have any specific safety tips?

Bob: They use their end caps a lot of times, which are displays at the end of the aisles. They'll use the end caps to get an item they want to get moving. But those key spots, they try to stock them up too much. Sometimes the end caps are built into pyramids, and employees take their razors and just cut open the case—the side of the box—so that they're easily taken out. And the customer can get hit by the bottles if they all come down. But so can the employees. Anything that will hurt the public will hurt employees as well.

Adam: Have you seen any claims like that?

Bob: Yes. As a matter of fact, I was just asked on one; I'm an expert witness as well. The other thing is spills and cleaning them up. And the employees can injure themselves while they're trying to clean up the spill. You know, "Broken bottle in Aisle 4," so the guy's rushing over there. If a spill doesn't get cleaned up, the employee knows there's a possibility of having a customer accident and management is worried about the employee going in there and cleaning it up. But if the employee goes in there without the right tools, the right gloves, they can get cut—because there is broken glass on the floor from when that bottle hit the floor. Employees can be injured from that, or they can slip on the product that they're trying to clean up.

Adam: What are some of the common problems you see in restaurants?

Bob: Cuts. Cutting and butchering. And the people are not taught safe techniques. The way around that is with a Kevlar glove. Years ago in the meat industry, they wore a steel-mesh glove; very uncomfortable, very difficult to work with, but it kept them from cutting the tips of their fingers off. The Kevlar glove is the same material they use in bulletproof vests. It's a light knit, it's comfortable, and you can use it all day long. But if you go and slip with the knife, it won't cut through it.

Adam: Are dull blades an issue?

Bob: Yes, because they're not going to cut through right and they tend to deflect.

Adam: Do you have any safety tips regarding ladders?

Bob: We like the movable metal stairways with wheels. You've got to get one that's the right size.

Adam: Why do you like the movable metal stairways?

Bob: Because it's a stairway. It's got handrails on it, and it's easy to move—when you lift the bar, the wheels come down and you just roll it to the next spot. When you step down on the bar, the wheels come up and the feet come down. Now you've got a ladder that's all set up. It's not a ladder; it's stairs. The stairs have steps on them that are deep, and at the top, you have a platform.

Adam: Do you have any safety tips for wholesalers?

Bob: One is training on the loading-dock areas to keep them clean. It's constantly a problem because everything is palletized these days, and the pallets get chewed up by the blades of the forklifts. So they're constantly splintering. Everybody must know that if you see it—pick it up. And all of the Saran-wrap-type material that is put around the pallets becomes a problem because you can trip on it. Sometimes you can get this caught up in the wheels of the forklift, and when it gets to a point that it really binds, the forklift will stop short and you can go flying.

Adam: How about the stacking in the warehouses?

Bob: How the material is stacked and the condition of the racks, because they get hit by the forklifts constantly, and they get bent. Racks were designed to hold weight when they were straight. The other thing I look at with rack storage is, is it bolted? I don't know how many places I've been in where management says, "We're not sure we like the way this rack system is set up, and that's why we didn't bolt it down." I say, "Well, you understand that the whole system can move if you don't have something to bolt." And they don't bolt it into concrete, or they don't bolt it enough. And management says, "Well that will be enough." Well, it really isn't. The manufacturer of the racks didn't say that you should bolt only every third row.

Adam: Do employers believe that many claims are fraudulent?

Bob: Some of the claims are. In some of them, the claimants were legitimately hurt, but they wanted to milk it. But if the accident didn't occur in the first place, then they couldn't be doing that. If employees know that you're going to do a thorough investigation of every single accident that occurs, that's a deterrent, and they're less likely to commit fraud.

Adam: Do you have any other money-saving ideas for employers?

Bob: If you can get an employer to get his or her employees to understand that he or she is concerned with their welfare and wants to provide a safe place to work, the number of accidents is going to be reduced. But it must come from the top down to get everybody on board. Then they've got to improve the work space.

If I've got everybody working in a dungeon, but I say I care about your welfare, I haven't sold it.

Adam: Why is it so important for employees to know that management cares?

Bob: Because they'll feel better about themselves. They'll work better. When they're told to do something, they won't ignore it. In other words, they know that they're hearing it because management doesn't want them to get hurt. Management legitimately cares. Management does this through a lot of different ways. They have a company picnic every year. They maybe have a Christmas party. That's to get everybody together to try to build some camaraderie, not for safety. Get the people to care about the company. Likewise, management needs to make the employees understand that they care about their safety and that the rules and regulations, the equipment guards, and the personal protective equipment they must wear are for the employees' safety.

Adam: Have you seen fewer claims at companies that demonstrate that they care about safety?

Bob: Generally, I would say, a good company that cares about employees' safety generally has a better safety record. But that's not necessarily going to reduce the number of accidents unless the company takes other actions. I mean the employer could care about employees. This company that I have that had the death case—I think that company truly cared about employees. They were very upset. They really liked the woman who died. She was thirty-seven years old.

Adam: What happened?

Bob: A pallet of tomato sauce—jarred tomato sauce—was stacked three high. Something happened with the second pallet, and nobody saw it, but part of it collapsed. This whole pallet came over and crushed the woman to death. She was working late, changing the labels on each of the pallets from white to pink because pink denoted organic and they were going to have an organic inspection the next day. She bent over next to this three-tier pallet—there was no evidence that this had happened and it had never happened before—but a pallet's made out of wood. Wood can collapse. It could have a fault in it. And that's what happened. And because of that fault, when the stack shifted, it came right over and fell on her.

Adam: Do you find that this issue of building a culture of caring is the most important thing you have to address?

Bob: You can have it that way, or you can have it the DuPont way. The DuPont way was "This is the way it's going to be done. It's tried; it's true. You'll do it, or you won't work here."

Adam: But behind that is…

Bob: Management cares.

Adam: Yes. They have to care enough to say that.

Bob: But if management gets it across to employees: "You want to work here; you're going to obey the rules." And the company needs a disciplinary policy that is clear and concise. "You will be given a warning, verbally, if you're doing something wrong. You don't have your safety glasses on. The second time, a written warning. Third time, you're going on suspension for a couple of days. Fourth time, you're never going to work here again. You're out the door."

Adam: Do you have any other suggestions?

Bob: The biggest thing regarding saving money is to look to what is a company's accident history and what they did after an accident occurred to prevent similar accidents from occurring again. It's not an overnight process. Management loves to see results. Sometimes it can take a year or two years to really start to develop programs that will work, and it's hard to keep management's attention.

Adam: Thank you, Bob.

Chapter 9

Interview with Eileen Preiato, Friedlander Claims Solution™ Manager

Eileen Preiato is a workers' compensation claims expert. She worked for more than twelve years with the Hartford Insurance Company, during which time she was the senior supervisor of the Workers' Compensation Claim Department, handling all aspects of claims from investigations to settlements. While with Hartford Insurance Company, she also was the hearing representative, handling hearings before the Workers' Compensation Board, and was later named assistant manager of their Westchester Claim Department Office. She later worked for more than five years for Empire Stat, reviewing Workers' Compensation claims at NYSIF for independent medical evaluations. In 2006, she joined the

Friedlander Group's Worker's Compensation Department as the senior claims solution adviser.

Adam: Eileen, what are the best methods that employers can use to reduce their workers' comp. costs?

Eileen: First, they need to make sure that they report claims timely, to avoid causing any delay for their employee and causing them hardship. They want to ensure prompt payment of the employee's benefits.

Adam: How does that help employers?

Eileen: Well, it helps employers because they won't have an employee who is now disgruntled since he or she is losing time from work, has no income, feels that no one cares, and feels neglected. If the claim is promptly reported, the benefits can be paid sooner, and the employee won't be hounded by people who are calling, saying, "You haven't paid this bill yet." It just helps create a better relationship with the employer and the employee, and it helps save money in that it helps get them back to work sooner.

Adam: Have you seen employers reaching out having a favorable impact on employees?

Eileen: Yes, definitely. When they see that the employer is reaching out, trying to make sure that they are taken care of, the employees are appreciative. If they're losing time, and the employer calls and contacts them, finds out how they're feeling, shows interest in the care they're receiving, asks if there is anything they're having issues with and if they're getting their comp. payments, this means a lot to injured employees. Being proactive creates that environment where the employee feels that the employer is taking an interest and is making sure that he or she is being taken care of. That helps foster a relationship where the employee wants to get back to work, rather than take advantage of the system and hurt the employer.

Adam: Do you have examples of employees that returned to work sooner due to a caring employer?

Eileen: There was a case where an employee found out that an MRI of his knee would be needed. The employer immediately made calls to find out how to get this authorized, which was done. The MRI showed that surgery would be needed, and again, the employer pursued the doctor to get the needed report and the carrier to get the surgery authorized. The result was the employee got the needed care in a very short time and was back to work in a much shorter time. The employee expressed that if not for the employer's efforts on his behalf, he would have been out of work for a longer time, and he was anxious to get back to work. This case is one example of the positive effects an employer has by being proactive for employees: everyone wins!

Adam: What else can employers do?

Eileen: Make sure that employees are receiving what they should, keeping the communication open is a very big plus, and reaching out to make sure that the employee knows that the employer is concerned and wants the employee back to work as soon as possible.

Adam: OK, what other ways can employers save money?

Eileen: Self-payment of eligible first-aid type bills is huge. It reduces the cost by keeping claims out of the system and their experience modification. It saves money for years.

Adam: How do you determine whether a bill can be paid by the employer?

Eileen: Under the workers' compensation law in New York, if you have no more than two visits to a doctor or no more than one working shift missed beyond the working day or shift on which the accident happened, employers do not have to report the claim to the Compensation Board and they can pay the bills themselves. Once it goes beyond that, they have to report it.

Adam: If a doctor bills $1,000, but the workers' compensation medical fee schedule only allows $150, how much does the employer have to pay?

Eileen: The amount on the schedule, $150. This issue comes up all the time because a lot of hospitals and doctors are saying that if you're self-paying, then you're not entitled to the workers' comp. fee schedule rate, which is not the case. Regardless of whether the carrier or the employer pays the bill, the amount due is at the lower fee schedule rate, which is part of the workers' compensation law.

Adam: Do you feel that your communication with employees gets them back to work sooner because they know someone's watching?

Eileen: Yes, I do think so. When employees know that the employer is actively following their progress as to when their next doctor's appointment is and what treatment they are receiving, it has been my experience that the majority of these employees return to work sooner. There is also the practice of having employees bring the employer a note from the doctor after the doctor's visit as to their degree of disability. I have found this face-to-face contact and interaction have a positive effect in getting the employee back to work.

Adam: How do you help employees return to work as soon as possible?

Eileen: Some employers are willing to allow employees to return to lighter-duty work, which we help coordinate. Let's say an employee worked in the warehouse packing boxes. If offered a temporary desk job, maybe answering phones or helping out doing customer service, the employee can return sooner. It gets them back into the workforce and out of the mode of sitting in front of the TV, having nowhere to go that day. So, even if the employee goes in for a few hours, you're reconnecting them with fellow workers. The employee is back in that working mode and is getting in the right frame of mind to return to work, once approved medically. And it's good for the employer because the other employees see that while the employee couldn't do any heavy lifting, their employer cared and was willing to find something for him or her to do, so that the employee wasn't losing any more time.

Adam: The sooner the employee returns to work, the more productive the employer?

Eileen: Right. And the employer has the employee, which is a valuable asset, back at work.

Adam: Have you helped employers keep off-the-job injuries from being reported as workers' compensation claims and ultimately increasing experience modifications?

Eileen: Yes, many times. For example, if an employer calls and says to us, "An employee had a bad cold, a fever, and passed out," that's not job related. He could have been sitting in his living room and passed out. Most employers assume that since it was on the job, we had to report it as a workers' compensation claim. So it works, but we need to catch the claim before it gets reported as a compensation claim, which is then difficult to reverse.

Adam: How can an employer know whether a claim is a disability claim under New York Disability Benefits Law or a workers' compensation claim?

Eileen: Well, a workers' compensation claim has to arise out of the course of employment and be caused by something job related. The fact that a person has a heart attack on the job doesn't always mean it arose because of his or her employment. The person might have had a heart attack anywhere. What the claimant has to prove is that it was due to the job and arose out of the course of employment. I have a recent claim where an employee was driving a truck and ran off the road, and it turned out he had a massive heart attack. So, the question was, would he have had that heart attack regardless of the fact that he was in the truck? The insurance carrier is contesting the claim. According to the doctor, the employee had heart disease, and it just so happened that he was in the truck when he had the heart attack.

Adam: What should employers do if they feel a claim is fraudulent?

Eileen: Employers need to let the carrier know that they think a claim is fraudulent as soon as possible. The wording on the C-2 claims form should say that "the employee alleges that…" This immediately puts a red flag on that C2 that the injury is questionable and that the employer does not confirm, did not witness the event, nor attests to its validity. The employer should document.

In other words, if there's something right away that the company feels is questionable, get the names of people with information. Get them to write out what they saw or didn't see or what they heard the employee say, such as saying at his or her coffee hour, "They're not giving me the days off I want, so I'm going to trip this afternoon." If someone overheard something like that, you want to get it all written down. So, the employer should immediately get evidence that may prove fraud.

Adam: Do you see retaliatory claims against employers?

Eileen: Yes. I've seen where employees have put in for a leave of absence or they put in for vacation time, and the employer said, "You know, sorry, you're not entitled to the time because you're not here long enough." Then, the next day, all of a sudden, the employee comes back and says, "I was lifting upstairs and now my back's out, and I can't work."

Adam: What will the carrier do with the information?

Eileen: The carrier will send out an investigator, get statements from the employer, anyone on the premises that has any information to gather, and try to get a statement from the claimant as to what he or she alleges happened.

Adam: What are proactive employers doing?

Eileen: Some employers are putting up posters that inform employees that fraud is a felony and punishable with jail time. These posters can be an effective deterrent.

Adam: Sometimes there are large medical expenses with fraudulent claims; does that mean the doctor was an accomplice?

Eileen: Not necessarily. The doctor may not be aware that the claim is fraudulent. If the employee alleges a back injury, it's very subjective. If you say to the doctor, "It hurts here, it hurts there, and I can't bend over," the doctor is responding to the complaints. There are claims for the same employer where you see everyone goes to the same doctor and everyone is disabled. No one ever gets better with this doctor. Or you see the same doctors hooked up with the same attorneys. Or, all of a sudden, a claimant changes doctors when he or she engages an attorney—things like that.

Adam: You've seen that?

Eileen: Yes, unfortunately, you do see things like that happening too often.

Adam: What is the most prevalent type of fraudulent claim?

Eileen: I think Monday morning injuries are the most questionable or first day back from vacation or a day off, but you have to realize these type of claims are very hard to prove unless you have solid evidence such as a video or a co-worker willing to testify.

Adam: So what can an employer do?

Eileen: Well, in that case, the carrier needs to investigate. The carrier does activity checks, and if they don't find the claimant home during the day, then they set up surveillance. In some cases, the employee posts videos on his or her Facebook page that show the claimant doing activities that prove the fraud.

Adam: Have you seen video surveillance work?

Eileen: Yes, they definitely have caught fraudulent claims. There was one where the claimant was collecting compensation benefits, and detectives caught him leaving every morning going to work in a deli in the next town over, and they followed him. He was arrested. There was a claim with a woman who worked in a hospital and she was collecting compensation. While collecting, she worked at a doctor's office and was fraudulently filling out her own medical reports of injury. She was doctoring her own medical reports to keep compensation checks coming her way.

Adam: What are your most memorable achievements with respect to claims?

Eileen: There are times when you really feel that you are making a difference, and a recent case comes to mind. An employee had severed a nerve and tendon on his thumb the Tuesday before Thanksgiving, and unless the hospital had the claim number and authorization that day, surgery could not be done until after the holiday. I was able to get this done in a few hours, and the surgery was done the next morning. The outcome may not have been as good if he had to wait. It is always rewarding when you are able to help guide the employers in reporting and explaining the workers' compensation law and work with them to get the benefits processed for their employees as soon as possible.

Adam: Thank you, Eileen.

Chapter 10

Interview with Cosmo Preiato, Head of Friedlander Group Safety Groups

Cosmo Preiato began his career in the insurance industry in January 1976. He started as a commercial lines underwriter for Country Wide Brokerage in New Rochelle, New York. In July 1977, Cosmo joined Friedlander Company, my father's insurance agency, as the commercial lines manager. After the formation the workers' compensation safety groups starting in 1992, Cosmo was promoted to executive vice president of Friedlander Group. Cosmo is head of Underwriting and Operations.

Adam: How can employers save money on their workers' compensation?

Cosmo: Well, employers need to have the employees properly classified, that's number one. If they don't, and they purposely mislead the carriers and misclassify the employees so they can pay a lower premium, it's a felony in the State of New York, and you could go to jail very easily. But if you have office workers who work in a fully enclosed office with a closing door, you can save a lot of money by classifying them as clerical workers, rather than as retail, wholesale, restaurant, or hotel classifications, which are much higher.

Adam: A clerical employee has a rate of one-third of a percent of payroll?

Cosmo: Yes.

Adam: If an employee is in a store, for example, and they have a separate office with a door, that employee qualifies for the clerical rate?

Cosmo: That's correct.

Adam: But if the employee has a desk in the back of the store, is the employee going to be charged at the higher store rate?

Cosmo: That is correct. It's got to be a regular office, where you have people sitting at desks doing phone work, typing, and engaging in clerical duties in general. That's all they are allowed to do. If they are also used occasionally to go work on the floor, in the store setting or a restaurant setting, the rules are that you cannot divide the payroll. That employee's payroll has to be put into the highest rated class, which, in this case, would be the store or the restaurant, or whatever the operation consists of.

Adam: If an owner of a store, with an office, talks with the customers in the store, the owner is going to be charged at the full store rate?

Cosmo: That is correct, for 100 percent of the payroll, subject to the minimum or maximum allowed.

Adam: Is it also true that if employers have someone who works in a wholesale warehouse, let's say, but does infrequent contracting work at a customer's location, that employee's payroll will be included in the contracting code, which would be quite a bit higher?

Cosmo: If that is the higher rate, that is correct.

Adam: How do officers qualify for the low officer rate?

Cosmo: Well, they have to do strictly administrative work; they cannot be involved in any day-to-day operation, such as going to the warehouse or the store or the restaurant, they have to work basically as a clerical person. Sit at your desk, do administrative work through the phone, and work through your supervisors; you don't deal directly with the rest of the employees and you are not exposed to the same elements as your general workers are.

Adam: If you have several classes of employees with varying rates, is it important to carefully classify the payroll to avoid overcharging on audit?

Cosmo: That is correct, and that really holds true when you're talking about fuel oil dealers that have drivers who deliver; then you have contracting employees who do the boiler installations and repairs; then you also have your clerical, outside salesmen, supervisors who work strictly from their desks; other supervisors who oversee employees in the field; and maintenance people. So, those supervisors that work from their desks and supervise via phone or e-mail, they will be classified as clerical, because they are not out in the field and not doing any direct supervision. And then you have the supervisors who are out in the field, and because they are essentially exposed to the same elements that the contractor employees are, they are going to be classified on the same level as the contractors. So, it's very important that you keep strict records as to which employees are assigned to what duties and that you make that information available to the auditors when they come out.

Adam: What do employers need to know about tracking overtime?

Cosmo: With overtime, you are charged the straight time portion of the overtime, not the overtime additional pay. For example, if the regular pay is $10 an hour, and the overtime pay is $15 an hour, on the overtime payroll, you pay premiums on $10; you don't pay premiums on the extra $5 overtime pay, but you have to have the records to reflect the overtime. The auditor must see those records.

Adam: What audit problems do you see?

Cosmo: Sometimes in certain cases, like the restaurants, if the employer doesn't have certain documents available to the auditor, and the auditor goes strictly off the New York Tax Return, the NYS45s, the employer is going to pay premiums inclusive of tips. So, if you don't present your Federal Tax Forms 941 to the auditor, where the tips are properly split out, you're going to be charged on those tips, and depending on the type of operation, it could be a lot of money. Tips should not be included in premium calculations.

Adam: What other areas would you advise the employer to focus on to reduce workers' compensation costs?

Cosmo: Obviously, safety is a very important issue. Employers must make sure that their employees have proper equipment and training. Hopefully that will reduce their claims, which will ultimately be reflected in their experience modification savings. So the fewer claims they have, the lower premium they will pay. This is something that they control.

Adam: You must see hundreds of employers that don't qualify for premium savings programs because their claims are too high.

Cosmo: That is correct. Claims will ultimately determine their acceptability into a better company, a lower-priced company, or in our case, safety groups. We look at claims history very closely.

Adam: Do you see audit issues often?

Cosmo: Well, in some cases, as we pointed out, an employer may have missed the overtime because the employer didn't have it prepared properly, so when the auditor comes out, they get hit with that additional payroll. As I mentioned before about restaurants, if tips aren't split out, that's going to hurt the employer, and that's a substantial amount, especially if you're talking about a larger restaurant where the employees are very dependent on the tips. We also have issues where employers feel that certain employees are misclassified. In their minds, they are clerical people, but the carrier has put them into the governing code, which could be warehouse, retail, or whatever their operation consists of. We guide the employer to put in writing exactly what the issues are, and we present it to the auditing department. If the auditing department agrees, they will make the adjustment. For example, an auditor told a hotel employer that they cannot have clerical people and must include them in the much higher hotel classification.

We told the employer to send us a letter indicating who the employees were and their salaries because the auditor was wrong. Based on that letter, we were able to get an audit adjustment done immediately because the supervisor at the State Fund totally agreed that the audit was incorrect.

Adam: Are there different rules regarding the various corporate structures?

Cosmo: Payroll is payroll. The only difference is that with a corporation, you cannot exclude any of the executive officers if you have more than two and if those two don't own 100 percent of the outstanding stock. So, if you have two executive officers who, together, own 90 percent, but the wife owns 10 percent but she is not in the office, you cannot exclude them. You may want to consolidate the ownership if you want to be excluded from the policy. Especially if you're working in the warehouse and your payroll is being charged at the warehouse rate. With respect to limited liability companies, all members are automatically excluded unless they elect to be included, in which case they would still be subject to the minimum and the maximum, the same as the corporate officers are. The same would apply to a limited partnership, a partnership, and a sole proprietor. They are all automatically excluded, but they can elect, in writing, to be included. If you're a sole proprietor working as a contractor, you may want to be included

Appendix

The Friedlander Group
Claims Solution™

This appendix is included to provide employers with an idea of potential services available in the marketplace.

Our unique process, The Friedlander Group Claims Solution,™ enables clients to maximize their productivity, efficiencies, and profits (PEP) by keeping their number one asset, their employees, working. That's the ultimate benefit of creating a Culture of Care™ company. Additional savings are captured from low experience modifications, large advance discounts, and dividends.

The fact that the safety groups managed by Friedlander Group have averaged 36 percent dividends since 1992 is proof positive that safety and effective claims administration work. Our laser focus on PEP maximization and our passion for helping clients win their World Series further improves results.

The Friedlander Claims Solution™ is a service offered to any employer in need of a partner to help them maximize their PEP.

First, we act as the outsourced claims administrator. We professionally manage the entire claims process. We streamline the reporting of claims, guide on self-payment, coordinate early-return-to-work programs, communicate with employees and advocate for them, hold employees accountable, and communicate with employers, employees, doctors, and the insurance carrier.

The larger an organization, the more overwhelming it can be with regulatory compliance and the onerous paperwork. Large organizations appreciate an outsourced administrator most. They're generally not staffed with the people who have the expertise to handle the process. By outsourcing the claims administration, clients save on payroll and experience modifications and can focus on their core business and strengths.

Reducing safety group claims is in the shared interests of members and the Friedlander Group. Friedlander seeks safety-conscious members that have low claims. When we apply the Friedlander Claims Solution,™ we reduce reserves and drive down experience modifications, which increases safety group profits that are paid as dividends to members. An outstanding 36 percent average dividend history since 1992 enables us to attract and retain additional safety-conscious members. We call this the Win-Win Alignment.™ It's unique in the industry.

Where possible, we encourage the employer to self-pay small first-aid type claims and use a proprietary No-Lost-Time Claims Form, when C-2 forms are not required. It saves money for the employer and reduces experience modifications and paperwork. Friedlander Group provides guidance to the employer, follows up on claims and payments, and calculates the reduced workers' compensation medical fee. It's usually a fraction of what's actually billed by the medical provider. This valuable service is a small example of what can be achieved with partners who offer specialized services.

Contrast that with a standard carrier that requires the C-2 claim form reported on every claim, which is not legally required. This increases claims' reserves and experience modifications. The insurance carrier receives additional premium and profits, but what does the insured get? The bill.

Our Self-Imposed Deductible Technique™ has saved clients thousands of dollars. For example, an employer was billed $1,251.90 for a hospital emergency-room visit. Because the claim was eligible, we recommended that the employer pay the bill rather than report it to the carrier. The reserve on that claim would have been higher as would the ultimate additional premium. Of the $1,251.90 billed, the New York State Medical Fee Schedule allowed only $101 for those services, which the employer gladly paid. They potentially saved thousands because their experience modification was not adversely affected and time was saved.

Another unique service included in our Claims Solution™ is our Executive Claim Prevention Report.™ This proprietary quarterly report isolates patterns by sorting each claim by cause. At a glance, an employer is enabled to eliminate patterns of unsafe acts and conditions causing their claims. The report enhances the effectiveness of the employer's Safety Committee by providing actionable data.

Our Return to Work Expeditor™ is designed to get injured employees back to work to maximize PEP. We consult with the employee, the employer, and the doctor to achieve the shared objective. We explore light-duty options.

The fact is that the longer an injured worker remains out of work, the less likely he or she will return. That minimizes PEP.

Studies indicate that the sooner an employee returns to work, the better. There's less fraud, fewer legal problems, reduced training, better morale, lower premiums and improved productivity.

Companies that have provided return-to-work opportunities have realized a 20 percent to 40 percent savings in workers' compensation costs in addition to the costs of hiring and training replacement workers.

An oil dealer told me recently that it can take up to two years to train a new boiler technician. Imagine the cost of that. The experience modification implications are considerable, but the ancillary costs (training, rehiring, lower morale, and lost productivity, efficiencies, and profits) are bigger.

Since an "ounce of prevention is worth a pound of cure," we leverage the Friedlander Safety Bank Account™ to help members prevent claims from occurring. Members are encouraged to "withdraw" a wide range of excellent tools that improve safety and build a Culture of Care.™

The goal is for top management to consistently communicate to employees that they are committed to safety, in both word and deed. Employees should go home from work in the same health in which they arrived. That's the key to success with workers' compensation. A company's claims experience is a footprint that shows whether management is "walking the walk."

Companies that invest in educating their employees benefit many times over. An excellent educational resource is provided by the AMCOMP – WCP Certification Program. More information can be found at www.amcomppro.com.

For companies that want to maximize their PEP, we provide on-site loss control, guidance on establishing and running safety committees, methods to communicate that management cares about safety, and free safety videos, posters, and training. We provide free on-site seminars and loss-reduction engineering that isolates and eliminates unsafe acts and conditions.

NYSIF has excellent online resources at http://ww3. nysif.com/AboutNYSIF/OnlinePublications.aspx. For example, you can download the comprehensive NYSIF guide, *Partners in Safety*, which discusses management leadership, establishing a safety culture and emergency planning. Download free safety posters at http:// ww3.nysif.com/SafetyRiskManagement/OnlineSafety Resources/SafetyPosters.aspx.

Some employers are really into safety, and we customize our services to support and add value to their efforts. "Continuous Improvement" is a core value of Friedlander Group.

Another service we provide is the Experience Modification Premium Recapture Method.™ This service corrects reserving errors on the prior seven years of claims. We retroactively reduce the prior three years of experience modifications and recapture premium savings.

We also provide employers with a customized three-year cost of various losses and their "controllable mod." Once they see what their claims are costing them and their controllable savings, they are motivated to take action and invest in safety. The return on investment is phenomenal.

About the Author

Adam Friedlander is the president of Friedlander Group, Inc., the workers' compensation leader for retailers, wholesalers, restaurants, hotels, and oil dealers in New York. Adam started his career in insurance in 1983, working with his father, Bert Friedlander. Bert began his career in the insurance industry working with his father, Harold Friedlander. In 1985, Adam bought his own agency, and in 1992, the Friedlander Group formed the first of five workers' compensation safety groups.

Adam has published several articles on insurance and group self-insured workers' compensation trusts.

Contact information:

Friedlander Group, Inc.
Adam Friedlander
2500 Westchester Ave., Suite 400A
Purchase, New York 10577
914-694-6000, ext. 206
adamf@friedlandergroup.com
www.friedlandergroup.com
http://www.linkedin.com/in/friedlanderadam
Twitter: @friedlanderadam

11421277R0010

Made in the USA
Lexington, KY
03 October 2011